# FULFILLING YOUR SPIRITUAL PROMISE

Volume 1

# FULFILLING YOUR SPIRITUAL PROMISE

## VOLUME 1

# JOHN-ROGER, D.S.S.

Mandeville Press
Los Angeles, California

Mandeville Press
P.O. Box 513935
Los Angeles, California 90051-1935
323-737-4055
jrbooks@mandevillepress.org
www.mandevillepress.org

Printed in the United States of America
ISBN 978-1-893020-17-7

# Other Books by John-Roger

*Blessings of Light*
*The Consciousness of Soul*
*Divine Essence*
*Dream Voyages*
*Forgiveness—The Key to the Kingdom*
*God Is Your Partner*
*Inner Worlds of Meditation*
*The Journey of a Soul*
*Living Love from the Spiritual Heart*
*Loving Each Day*
*Loving Each Day for Moms & Dads*
*Loving Each Day for Peacemakers*
*Manual on Using the Light*
*Momentum: Letting Love Lead* (with Paul Kaye)
*Passage Into Spirit*
*The Path to Mastership*
*The Power Within You*
*Psychic Protection*
*Relationships: Love, Marriage and Spirit*
*Sex, Spirit and You*
*The Spiritual Family*
*Spiritual High* (with Michael McBay)
*The Spiritual Promise*
*Spiritual Warrior: The Art of Spiritual Living*
*The Tao of Spirit*
*Walking with the Lord*
*The Way Out Book*
*Wealth & Higher Consciousness*
*What's It Like Being You?* (with Paul Kaye)
*When Are You Coming Home?* (with Pauli Sanderson)

*To all the Beloveds*
*fulfilling their spiritual promise*
*and going Home to God*

# CONTENTS

# Volume 1

CONTENTS

# Volume 2

# CONTENTS

# Volume 3

CONTENTS

# Contents

# FOREWORD

I have studied with John-Roger—and, frankly, I've studied John-Roger—for forty years or so. In the late 1960's, I began working with him and assisting him to transform his spoken teachings into the written word, the better to reach people who were looking for a light in their lives. It is heartening beyond words to see a book such as this one available to readers because it gathers so much of John-Roger's wisdom into one tome.

When I say I have studied John-Roger for forty years, what I mean is that he has intrigued me from the first day I met him and, after all these years, intrigues me still. He is an absolute original, one-of-a-kind masterpiece. Very often, he is a surprise. He is a mystic and has lived a life profoundly grounded in Spirit and in service. He is completely spontaneous and unpredictable, which I have come to believe is the result of following a free and unpatterned Spirit. He is the most loving human being I have ever encountered—and undoubtedly the funniest. His teachings are a curious blend of Eastern and Western thought. As you read his works, you will find teachings of reincarnation, the laws of karma (cause and effect), the evolvement of individualized consciousness through realms of Spirit, the grace bestowed on humankind by Christ, forgiveness, the power of working with the Light of the Holy Spirit, the use of mantras, the chanting of God's sacred names, and the benefits of meditation all woven seamlessly together to create a tapestry—and within that tapestry may be found a path that J-R calls Soul Transcendence, a path by which you may fulfill your spiritual promise.

I've heard John-Roger refer to himself as a spiritual scientist, meaning he is pragmatic and checks out everything he teaches to be sure it is workable (it is). And I've heard him say he teaches "practical spirituality" (he does). One of his favorite sayings is, "If it works, use it; if it doesn't work, let it go." Through the years, I've heard him answer innumerable questions with one of his own: "Did it work for you?" Other times, he shares—from the generosity of his loving heart—information that is both practical and liberating. Whatever his response, his answers are accompanied by an infusion of spiritual

energy that is, in itself, transforming. I've sometimes not understood anything of what he said, but
whatever was bothering me disappeared. There is
something mystical in the energy he works with
that takes his words beyond the mind and into the
heart and Soul. I think of it as a little bit of magic,
and it keeps me mindful that there is more to this
than meets the eye.

Much of what you read here (and in other books
by John-Roger) is the result of his response to people's desire to get free, to break the bonds of negativity that hold them down, to realize the positive side
of their nature. Someone says, "I just keep doing the
same stupid things over and over," and J-R says, "Let
me tell you about karma and how to break the
cycle." Another student says, "I am so angry at my
parents that it affects everything I do," and J-R says,
"I'll tell you about using forgiveness as a path to liberation." Someone else says, "Nothing seems to work
very well for me," and he says, "Here are some ideas
about working with the Light." Add it all together
and you get the science of Soul Transcendence, your
practical guide to fulfilling your spiritual promise—
and a bit of mystery to keep you intrigued.

From the altitude of the mystical consciousness,
I believe it must be clear that each person is the

embodiment of a divine Soul and that each Soul knows its own destiny and path back into its true nature. I say this not from any mystical conscious-ness of my own, but from my observations that it is from that premise that J-R treats all of his family, friends, students, acquaintances, the guy at the carwash, the waitress in the local diner, and the down-and-out fellow on the street corner. On some level, we are all the same and he knows it, so we are all awarded the same respect, love, and neutral regard. As a personal friend, student, and acquain-tance of J-R's, and a sometime waitress and even occasional car washer for him (and maybe down but never out), I can say that I have always experi-enced myself honored by him as a creative, unique, and individual Soul on a human path. Just that has encouraged me to grow, reach into new ventures, find my way in this sometimes difficult world, behave in ways more courageous than I actually felt, and risk loving myself and others in greater and greater ways.

Another thing I have learned from studying John-Roger (and his teachings) is that God wants us to succeed and to be happy. I have watched him be successful, happy, abundant, joyful, and free. And his teachings encourage us to do the same. In this book, you will find many practical tips and hints for living life in a more fulfilling way. I invite you to experiment. See if anything here works for you. Practice observation. Pause from time to time and ask yourself, "Did that work for me?" and you'll find yourself becoming your own spiritual scientist. And you may find yourself fulfilling your spiritual promise by awakening to the original, funny, free, creative, magical, mysterious masterpiece you are. And then, Soul Transcendence is just around the corner. John-Roger can be your guide.

Pauli Sanderson

# PREFACE

The biggest challenge in compiling this book was deciding what to put in it. John-Roger (J-R) has done over six thousand seminars and question-and-answer sessions and has published dozens of books, and he is still presenting more information even as this is written. So the question of what to include—and exclude—was a bit daunting. But the line had to be drawn somewhere, and we hope that *Fulfilling Your Spiritual Promise* gives you a good overview of many of J-R's teachings yet does not "strain your purse and sprain your wrists."

This book includes information from many sources, such as unreleased seminars and question-and-answer sessions, tapes and CDs currently available, J-R's articles in *The New Day Herald,* his answers to questions that people have asked him in letters, and some information in the wonderful early publications *The Journey of a Soul, Awakening into Light,* and *The Consciousness of Soul,* as well as the informative *Passage into Spirit.* There is some information from other sources, such as Appendix 2, An Informal History of MSIA. The full Glossary is at the end of each volume, and it defines many terms used in the book.

Designed primarily for the student in MSIA and useful for anyone wanting to know more about J-R's teachings, *Fulfilling Your Spiritual Promise* includes not only explanations of such broad concepts as karma and the human consciousness but also such specifics as how to dispose of a person's MSIA materials after death. One rule of thumb for inclusion of material was, "Would I have wanted to know this when I first started studying in MSIA?"

That said, the information in this book may represent a small part of what J-R has said on these topics. In addition, the Spirit is always free-flowing, found in the present moment and not "set in stone" in a book or other written form. The information in *Fulfilling Your Spiritual Promise* is meant to provide a start, a direction to look in, and we encourage people always to look within themselves for Spirit's direction. And when reading the book, you might bring to it an intention to awaken more to the Spirit. This can be like a prayer to God to reveal Itself to you, and the outer information may trigger an awakening to the living teachings of the spiritual heart.

Throughout, there are suggestions of J-R's books, audio seminars, and video seminars that give additional information on the topics covered. We can't urge you strongly enough to go to these other materials—the audio and video seminars, books, and especially the Soul Awareness Discourses, which are the Mystical Traveler's teachings on the physical level.

We think the material in this book is both useful and interesting. The information in later chapters does build on what is explained in earlier chapters, so you may want to read the book from the beginning, but it's not at all necessary to do that. You can also use it as a reference book for individual subjects you want to explore, and the expanded Contents pages and the Index (both of which are in all three volumes) can help you access what you want to read about.

At the same time, there is a difference between just *reading* the information and *studying* the information. We encourage you to actively engage with the information, apply what you read, and see how it works in your life. J-R teaches Soul Transcendence, which is becoming consciously aware of oneself as a Soul and as one with God, and he has said that the Soul is the spark of the Divine in each person. As you engage with the Soul consciousness through these teachings, your Soul can awaken, and this is not from a theory or speculation but from your own experience.

J-R has often commented that joy is an indication of Spirit's presence, and in so many of his seminars and sharings, there are eruptions of laughter and general hilarity. So, to get a wonderful taste of that joy of the Spirit, we highly recommend that you listen to what J-R says is his favorite seminar: "The Traveler—The One Who Laughs in Your Heart."

Enjoy!

Betsy Alexander

ह्रू

This is the Sanskrit symbol for Hu, which
is one of the names of God chanted in
MSIA.

# ACKNOWLEDGMENTS

My thanks to the following people, who contributed to the creation of *Fulfilling Your Spiritual Promise:* John Morton, for his idea of doing a book like this; Betsy Alexander, compiler and editor; David Sand, book design; Clea Rose and Lisa Liddy, production; Vincent Dupont, project coordinator; Virginia Rose, editorial assistant; Janis Hunt Johnson and Stephen Keel, copyeditors; Andrée Leighton, Munyin Choy-Hallinan, Valerie Peake, Nancy O'Leary, and Carrie Hopkins-Doubts, proofers; Joanne Sprott, indexer; Stede Barber, drawings of the Disciples; Ken Meyer, photo of John-Roger.

# A Word on Study Materials

There are some MSIA materials that are *only for the person receiving them,* and these include Soul Awareness Discourses and Soul Awareness Tapes/CDs (SAT series). These are not to be shared with anyone else. If you want to order a SAT selection, you need to be a SAT series subscriber.

There are also what we call *personal-use* audiotapes, CDs, videotapes, and DVDs. These may be shared with your spouse and children under 21 years old living at home.

Finally, there are *public-use materials.* All books (excluding Discourses) are public-use, and certain audiotapes, CDs, videotapes, and DVDs are also public.

All audio and video materials recommended in this book are designated as personal-use, public-use, or SAT. And for more information on the reasons for these designations, please see page 678.

To order any MSIA materials, you can contact MSIA:

P.O. Box 513935, Los Angeles, CA 90051
Phone: 323-737-4055
Fax: 323-737-5680
Internet: www.msia.org

झू

*You come into this world, attempting to fulfill certain qualities within yourself, and you go about it in many ways. But there is a prime directive that everyone works under:*

> *You are here to find out who you are, to find out where the Soul realm is and go there, and to have co-creative conscious-ness with God, the Supreme Father.*

*This is your whole direction and purpose on this planet. This is where your satisfaction and your ful-fillment lie. This is your spiritual promise.*

ध्रू

## CHAPTER 1

# INTRODUCTION

This is a book about love—the love that brought you here and the love that you are. It is about seeing through the eyes of the Soul, which see only love. It is about joy and using everything in your life for your upliftment, growth, and learning—because everything in your life *is* designed for that. It is all designed *for* you, personally, in the deepest and most profound way possible. And when you truly know that, you will live in freedom and the fulfillment of your spiritual promise.

There are three tenets we use in the Movement of Spiritual Inner Awareness (MSIA), and they are the foundation for this book and for everything I teach:

1. Out of God come all things.
2. God loves all of Its creation.
3. Not one Soul will be lost.

3

Let's briefly look at them.

*Out of God come all things.*

Spiritually, the same flow of energy that is going through you is going through me and through others. This is why Jesus said that "when you have done it to the least one of these, you have done it to me" (Matthew 25:40). Because all things come out of God, if we become prejudiced against one, we have become prejudiced against the awakening of our own consciousness of love.

*God loves all of Its creation.*

In the Bible, it says that after God created the world and human beings, He saw that it was very good. That means God loves it. God is maintaining us here and has also given us the ability to build and change according to our own will.

*Not one Soul will be lost.*

The Soul is the energy of God manifesting in the physical body. Since out of God come all things, God cannot lose Itself. People cannot lose their Soul, for how can anyone lose something that is immortal and that has always existed?

4

In MSIA, there are certain things that we keep in mind as we go through life, and they are our guidelines:

1. Don't hurt yourself and don't hurt others.
2. Take care of yourself so you can help take care of others.
3. Use everything for your upliftment, growth, and learning.

We also believe that God as Christ dwells within each person as a spirit and that we have to treat people in relationship to that spirit, which we discern as being a loving force. We feel that our job, then, is to become ministers to everyone in relationship to this Christ Consciousness, this loving feeling, no matter where we find anyone at any time. MSIA's teachings go into how we get in our own way, how to get out of our own way, and how to assist other people without inflicting on them or trying to ram a point of view at them.

This planet is a classroom, and each of us is here to gain experience and to become aware of the Divinity within ourselves—to awaken to and fulfill our spiritual promise. Your exploration of this can be a life-long adventure; it certainly has been—and

धू

*Work the new ideas that come your way. See what they do. You won't be deceived by anyone if you check things out.*

continues to be—for me. This book offers some outer ideas and support for your inner exploration of this.

Our primary approach is that each person needs to validate by their own experience the reality of the teachings. So, we do not deal in a strong belief-structure; rather, we encourage you to believe in your own experiences and what those experiences bring to you in terms of your inner awareness and inner enlightenment. And, of course, these are all very individual because not everyone approaches the teachings from the same background or context of life. The teachings are wide enough and volumi-nous enough so that most people can readily see within them how they can fulfill their life destiny more completely in terms of the spirit that they are. So this is my advice as you read this book: if it works for you, use it. If it does not work for you, have the wit to let it go, bearing in mind that this may change over time. What is working today may not work tomorrow, and, conversely, what does not work today may work for you tomorrow. So we strive to remain open to each new experience.

I am not bringing forward new information. I am bringing forward the ancient message that has been said over and over, and all I am doing is repeating it in words that are for our time. Sometimes I may get tired of repeating it, but I keep doing it anyway out of my loving for you. At some point, you will get tired of hearing me and you will start doing it for yourself, and that will be the day you awaken yourself. And if you sit down very quietly and tune in, you will get it from the Spirit within you, which is more effective anyway.

I am not asking you to believe what I say. I prefer not to speak to people who are believers, those who, if you say anything, just believe it. I like to have people bring their critical faculties with them, so as you read this, I would like you to bring your mind, your intelligence, and everything that you have heard or that you have been exposed to. Most of all, I would like you to have the experience of these things yourself.

You may read things that are new to you. You may also read things that you already knew but you did not know that anyone else knew them, and you will find them validated here. Some things may seem strange and peculiar, even "loony." In a way, they *are* loony, and this is because what we see physically is reflected light. You see something or someone else because they are reflecting light, but you see the Spirit because the Spirit Itself is shining. So the Spirit world is, in that sense, backwards from this world.

Years ago, some psychologists did an experiment where subjects wore glasses that reversed the vision from the right eye to the left eye and then upside down. So if a person tried to go right, according to what he saw, he would really have to go left. And if he saw something that he would normally have to reach down to get, he would have to reach up. Needless to say, the subjects were having a very hard time. As I watched this experiment, I said to myself, This is what it's like to be spiritual. This is why, when you go on a spiritual path, some people think you are crazy, no good, or even corrupt. But it is all cultural. If you were doing that in India, for example, there would be temples or ashrams into which you would fit just fine.

So as you read this book, try not to let your cultural background or the vocabulary get in your way. I go towards reaching the heart. I want your heart to come open because I have found that when your heart opens, you will have wisdom as a by-product of liking and loving. Then you get intelligence. Then the wisdom comes out, and from that comes the knowledge of how to do it again. It is what I call being a spiritual scientist. If you are really being religious—and "religious"

घू

*You are the Light. You are divine. You are in a*
*state of becoming aware of what you already are.*
*In your spiritual quest, look for love in all things.*

means to be realigned with God—then you are being a scientist, because the only way you can realign yourself is to stop the belief in what you think or what you have heard or read from others and, instead, find out for yourself.

Above all, look for the loving, which is how all of this works. Without love, no matter what else we have, it will not work. And if we have love, no matter what else we do not have, it *will* work.

ध्

## CHAPTER 2

# THE REALMS OF SPIRIT

*There is nowhere you can go that you are not in the body of God—nowhere. There is no place you can conceive or imagine that you are not within this frequency of Spirit. Even in your darkest moment, you are still in the body of God.*

## Introduction

You exist on many levels of consciousness at the same time. It can take a while to know this for yourself, and you will truly know through your *experience*. That experience can come through an intuitive flash, for example, but for most people it comes with continuous practice—and the most effective way of practicing I have found is spiritual exercises, an active form of meditation. (This is explained in chapter 9, Spiritual Exercises and Soul Transcendence.)

झू

*You must test the teachings to find out if they are true and valid for you. When you hear a teaching or message, you should always test it out.*

In this chapter, I will give the information I have gained through my own experience of going into the various realms of Spirit. I share it here not as something for you to memorize and learn only mentally but as background information that you can have in case you run across these things in your own "inner travels." It can also give you an inkling of how large and expansive your consciousness is. You can know these realms through your direct experience, at which point the information moves out of the theoretical area and becomes experiential.

This chapter is an overview of life in the Spirit, as I have seen it. I will present the information to you and show you how a lot of it interrelates. Then you have to realize that it is a "lie," although it is not meant to be a lie. I am really attempting to tell you the truth, but as soon as I talk about the invisible in terms of anything you can relate to in this world, you have to know that it is inaccurate because everything I say out of a physical body is an illusion. No matter how close I come to describing the spiritual levels, I cannot tell you how they really are because there are no words to describe what is going on there. And, as I said, your own experience of these realms will be the best validation you can have of their existence.

# Chart of the Realms #1

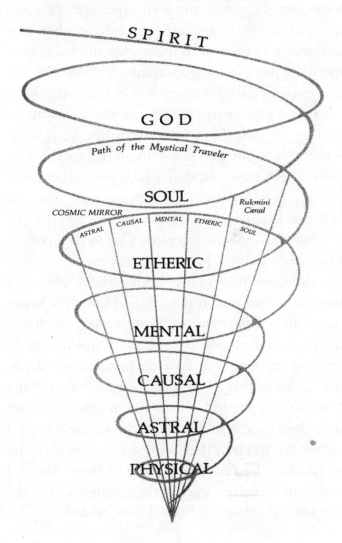

SPIRIT

GOD

*Path of the Mystical Traveler*

SOUL

*COSMIC MIRROR*

ASTRAL | CAUSAL | MENTAL | ETHERIC | SOUL

*Rukmini Canal*

ETHERIC

MENTAL

CAUSAL

ASTRAL

PHYSICAL

With that in mind, let's look at the realms of Spirit.

Physical realm (relating to the physical body, that which is material)
Astral realm (relating to the imagination)
Causal realm (relating to the emotions)
Mental realm (relating to the mind)
Etheric realm (paralleling the unconscious)
Soul realm (relating to who you really are)

These realms exist both *within* you (as your own levels of consciousness) and *outside* of you (as distinct realms of existence). They are not like stories in a building; rather, they are vibration rates, and each has characteristics, vibrations, and situations that are unique to it.

The Chart of the Realms #1 on page 16 shows the major realms. Note that the spiral going through all the realms is called the Path of the Mystical Traveler, indicating that the Traveler Consciousness is found in all the levels of existence. (For more on the Traveler, see chapter 7, Soul Transcendence: The Work of the Mystical Traveler.) As the chart indicates by the slanted vertical lines, in the physical realm, all the levels exist: physical, astral, causal, mental, etheric, and Soul. The other realms all have aspects of the astral, causal, mental, and etheric, and the Soul is also found there.

There are two important things to notice here. First, only in the physical level do all the levels exist at the same time. Second, the only aspect that is common to all levels is the Soul. The Soul is the most important aspect and carries through everything. In each of the levels, the Soul, the "I Am," resides all the time as an ongoing beingness, essence, consciousness. It has to be on all the levels because of its nature. It is who you are.

The physical, astral, causal, mental, and etheric realms are in the lower, or negative, planes of existence. "Negative" as I am using it here does not mean "bad" but, rather, negative like one of the poles of a battery. A battery has a negative pole and a positive pole, and together they create the charge that is the power. In a similar way, the planes of existence have negative and positive poles.

The Soul realm is the first of the positive realms of existence. There are also twenty-seven ascending realms of Spirit above the Soul realm. They are all involved in the greater, more conscious realization of Soul, God, and Spirit, until the Soul eventually dissolves its individuality into its greater oneness with the Supreme God of all. These realms of pure

Spirit defy explanation in physical vocabulary and must be experienced to be known. There are no words; it can only be said that they do exist and that it is everyone's potential and heritage to know of them someday in direct, conscious experience.

The Soul, expressing through various forms, may incarnate on any of these realms at various points in its journey. When the Soul incarnates on the physical realm, it has the unique opportunity of experiencing all of the negative realms simultaneously (that is, the physical, astral, causal, mental, and etheric). The Soul's experience on any negative realm other than the physical is more restricted or limited to that particular realm. But through the form of the human on the physical realm, the Soul's awareness is multidimensional, and the Soul can simultaneously experience all negative realms as well as all positive realms. This fact, alone, makes being in a physical body of great value spiritually, as I will explain below.

## Overview of the Realms

So let's start where you are now: the *physical*. From the Soul's point of view, the most important things about being on the physical level are that (1) the Soul is gaining experience here, and (2) this level

घु

*You are on all levels of Light. Right now, in this moment, you are already there. To be consciously aware of any or all of these levels, you need only expand the consciousness to encompass them. The way to expand the consciousness instantly is to move directly into the Soul, which has all vision, all knowledge.*

is a "springboard" into the Soul realm. It is only from the physical level that the Soul can move directly into the Soul realm and above. From any other lower realm—astral, causal, etc.—the Soul moves up level by level.

Above the physical realm is another world, the *astral* realm, which relates to the imagination and which is invisible in terms of the material world. The word *imagination* comes from the words *image in,* and to imagine is to take a thought or idea, put it in a form, and put it inside. Each of us, when we close our eyes, automatically goes into the astral level.

Above the astral realm is the *causal* realm, which refers to the emotions and is where the seeds of karma are. The Judeo-Christian idea that is equivalent to the idea of karma is "as you sow, so you reap" (Galatians 6:7). We often call the emotions the feelings, but emotions are really a contraction of these words: *energy in motion.* So when we are having emotions inside of us, we are actually having energy moving through us, or we are having energy blocked so that it has a very difficult time moving through us.

Above the causal realm is the *mental* realm. Sometimes we refer to this as the mind area. (It is not the brain; the brain routes information, and the mind is outside the brain.) Another word to describe the mental realm is *intellect*. This is what we get out here in the world from books, teachers, and so on. We put it in, memorize it, and put it back out. The Soul, in contrast, is intelligence. It just knows.

The realm above the mental is called the *etheric,* and it parallels the unconscious. This whole etheric is dark, and there is little or no awareness of it. In fact, there is a void at the top of it, through which we have to pass in order to get into the Soul realm. This void relates to our unconscious.

Above the etheric is the *Soul* realm, the first of the positive realms of Spirit. When we go to sleep, we may not go into the unconscious, as some people think. We may go into the Spirit. The Bible says that if you want to know God, worship God in the Spirit, that is, the Soul. (It did not say to worship God in the flesh.) The Soul is connected to the Spirit, and at that moment of being in the Soul, you can have total fulfillment and worship because you are spiritually alive.

MSIA teaches how to transcend across from the physical, the astral, the causal, the mental, the etheric, into the Soul and above.

## Coming into a Physical Existence

The Soul comes from and has its home in the Soul realm. It takes on a physical body and comes here to gain experience, and Earth provides many, many experiences.

As the Soul moves into a physical, material existence, it picks up an etheric body (sheath), which is a very fine substance that covers the Soul. As the Soul continues to descend, it picks up mental, causal, and astral bodies (sheaths), each one increasing in density. When "you" are born, it means that the Soul has picked up the densest sheath, the physical body.

You are probably very acquainted with the characteristics of the physical realm but may not be as familiar with the other realms, so I will give a brief explanation of each of them.

### Astral Realm

In the astral realm, as I have said, there are the astral, causal, mental, etheric, and Soul levels. And in the causal level of the astral realm, just as an example, there could be ten million levels. This levels-within-a-level-within-a-realm arrangement exists in all the realms, and there are truly "worlds without end."

The astral realm is where the imagination and concomitant feelings reside. Although there is no physical in the astral world, the astral body does resemble the physical body, but it is not in the condensed energy form of the physical body.

The astral body has a double body around it that has all our unconscious baggage of this world. Part of that package is everything that we have done and not done that is still hanging around us. Excess weight in the physical body is sometimes a direct result of undone things. We have tucked these "incompletes" into the baggage around us. As soon as we handle something, we often feel as if a load has lifted off our back, and we may also be in a position to lose weight physically and to lighten up emotionally, as well.

You cannot have physical experiences in the astral world, although if we were in the astral world right now and I offered you a glass of wine, it might taste better on that level because the senses are sharper there. In a strange sort of way, you might qualify as a better "wine taster" in the astral world than in the physical. If you are going to be a drunkard, perhaps the astral world is the best place. At least you cannot fall down physically; in the astral, it is more like floating.

24

Insomnia often comes from the mental level in the astral realm. The astral mind continually mentalizes about issues; combining with imagination, it affects the body and, at times, the adrenal glands, causing the nervous system to react. If the pituitary gland has been involved in too much mentalizing, there is a stream of action from the mind with no apparent way to control it. One way to handle this situation is to get out of bed and do some exercise that is strenuous for you. This will use the excess adrenaline in the body, and you may then be able to lie down and rest.

Most psychics function from the astral level, which is a level of phenomena, levitation, and table-raising. This realm of imagination has a powerful influence on the physical realm, and these kinds of phenomena feed off the imagination.

Most dreams occur in the astral level. Another way we imagine, or image-in, is by daydreaming. Daydreams actually weave in and out of the astral, causal, and physical worlds. Daydreaming is not necessarily a waste of time. For example, it can be quite useful for giving a person time to manage their emotions through getting away from a source of emotional difficulty. Daydreaming also permits the creative elements to fuse and produce more easily without the conscious self (a person's usual, everyday self), ego, and judgment in the way. Part of the creative process involves putting those aspects aside so that the creative forces can flow freely. The structuring comes in later when you translate the vision into something tangible. Einstein daydreamed, as did Edison and many other creative, inventive people. Adults often do not feel comfortable calling it daydreaming, however, so we invented another, more mature word—*preoccupation*. Children often daydream, and when a student is daydreaming in class, instead of saying to stop it, a better approach is for the teacher to ask the student to write or draw what they are seeing.

In the astral realm, there are so many unanswered prayers, and it would stagger you to see the junk that is there. If someone has prayed for a refrigerator and they stopped short of getting it, it is still there. The same with cars, hospitals, fundraising events, marriages, "Soul mates," what have you—it is really junky up there. If you did not get it, you have to clean up your creation because, as Jesus said, "Ye are gods" (John 10:34), and a god is responsible for its creation.

To clean it up, you have to consciously "cancel the order" and stop putting energy into it. "But," you might ask, "what about all those things I asked for before I knew how this works?" If you do not remember them, you can ask God that they be released and returned to the nothingness from which they came. You can also do free-form writing to get them out (see Appendix 1 for an explanation of how to do this). And if you are working with the Mystical Traveler, much of this can be cleared in the sleep state and through grace.

The Lord of the astral level is more brilliant than sixteen suns. St. Peter, often called "the gatekeeper," is in the astral realm, and the top part of the astral realm, called Summerland, is what most Christian religions and other orthodox religions call heaven. You may live here 1,500 years and have to turn away from the Lord of the astral level because its reflection would be so bright—and that is still in the psychic-material worlds. Even though you might think you are in heaven eternally, you will generally return to a physical, material existence.

## Causal Realm

The Lord of the causal realm (often called Jehovah) is at least a thousand times more brilliant than the Lord of the astral realm. In terms of the creation of the world, Jehovah's job was to build this

घू

*This physical level is the most insecure, the most doubt-ridden, and the most frustrating level, but that's because it is the classroom.*

particular planet and to work in this planetary system. Religions that originate from the causal realm are emotional in their form of worship and devotion. The Pentecostal churches, the Holy Rollers, the Quakers, the Shakers, the Roman Catholic Church, and many others draw their energy field from the Lord of the causal realm. This is not to place a value judgment on these groups, just to state their origin. People who are highly focused on working with emotions in their karmic flow are likely to be drawn to religions that come out of the causal realm.

The emotions can be seen as a thread that weaves throughout the entire fabric of our lives. On this thread resides our DNA and RNA programming of inherited predisposition towards the areas that we are here to balance in this existence. The "seeds of karma" and the records of all of our actions from all of our existences are kept in the causal realm. That is, the causes of the things that happen in this physical level originate in the causal realm, which is the level of cause and effect, and everything we have to work out in the world comes out of this realm. We may sometimes think that most of our troubles come from this level, but, from a higher perspective, any troubling situation is actually a balancing action.

The emotive body, which is in the causal area, produces emotional energy that has little if any intellect. As an analogy, water can be said to move in an energy pattern that has no intellect. The energy of the causal area that we call emotions carries us along and has no intellect.

How you act is always your choice. If you rely on the emotional energy and ride it like a flood or, in some cases, Niagara Falls, you can go with that energy. Or you can bring forth your intelligence to determine if you really want to go along with your emotions or if you want to just stand next to the observation railing, hold tight, and observe the emotions flooding by without participating in them. It can be difficult to do this, especially in the beginning, but it can get easier in time through practice.

## Mental Realm

Thinking is not a natural process of the human consciousness. You may say, "Sure it is; everybody thinks," but very few people actually think. Most people react and then pass that off as thinking. Thinking is the cause of things. Reaction is the effect. Most people think about 10 percent of the time and react the other 90 percent, and for the most part, people are reacting either to their previous reaction or someone else's reaction.

The inadequate use of the intellect by the human race after all the centuries of negative creation is something to behold. People still do not know that the mind has been placed with the physical body to help the Soul discern what is going on in the physical realm. The mind has to be a master dynamo to fulfill that function, and it is. As a creator, you have a challenge ahead of you: to create responsibly. Jesus once said, in essence, that you become what you think. He did not come out and say, "You draw energy fields to yourself and charge them with negativity or positivity." He used words that were applicable to the time and place in which he lived.

In working with the mind, it is important to remember this: energy follows thought. That means if you are thinking about a hot fudge sundae, all the levels of your consciousness come in line to bring that to you. The same is true for envisioning and moving towards higher spiritual awareness. All of your levels will start making that happen. That is why it is so important to watch your thoughts because you will create physically those things you have focused on in your thinking. Also, be careful of what you say. Listen to

ह्रू

*Thoughts cannot conceive the greatness of the
Soul. You can't find the majesty of the Soul in
science books or math books. You may not even
be able to consciously look and find a key that
awakens something inside of you a little more
than before. So all you can do is let go and say,
"It's beyond my mental ability."*

what you say and be sure it represents what you really want in your life.

At the same time, keep in mind that perfection is not achieved on the physical level. In the Soul, you are already perfect; everyone is. In the body, emotions, and mind, you are working to bring yourself into balance so that you can more readily see the Soul's perfection. And as you learn to keep yourself balanced, you can move out of the areas of dogma and opinion and move into a state of being. In that state, you will be aware of what is going on, but you will not necessarily have to enter into it. You will not have to get down in the "muck and mire" of negative expression. You simply keep yourself balanced and clear within your own consciousness, regardless of what is going on around you.

## Etheric Realm

Above the mental realm is the etheric realm, which parallels the unconscious. In this area, we may experience what we call goblins, ghosts, and "things that go bump in the night." We may also experience angels, beautiful devas, and ancient cities.

The etheric is one of the areas into which we repress our negativity. Everything that has not yet been cleared in the physical, astral, causal, and mental

घृ

*The more you can use every aspect of your existence as a spiritual exercise or as a spiritualized exercise, the more successful you will be in bridging into the etheric.*

levels gets projected onto the "cosmic mirror," which is at the top of the etheric realm and which divides this realm from the Soul realm. Your worst dreads, thoughts, feelings, and circumstances may all appear on the cosmic mirror as realities, but they are only reflections. The cosmic mirror may also reflect to you the glories of the earth. Then you may enter into an identification with that glory and reincarnate.

If you could look at these things clearly, they usually would not bother or entrap you, but in the etheric level, things are often misty and veiled because they are perceived through a swirling, dark void. One way to break through the realm of the unconscious into Soul is to work with one who has the keys, the knowledge, and the ability to show you the illusion of the unconscious and the way through it into the Soul. The Mystical Traveler Consciousness can do this.

By the time you evolve to the etheric realm, you have gone through the brilliance of the Lords of the astral, causal, and mental realms, and now you are reflected as the brightest thing in sight. The fact is, however, that you are still not in the Soul realm. Some people settle in the etheric realm, thinking this is heaven as they experience God's presence. God is, indeed, present in the etheric, as It is in all the other realms, but this is not the heaven that we

घू

*When you reach the Soul level, there is only a knowingness of God that does not rely on the body, mind, emotions, or imagination. It just is. In Soul awareness, there are no thoughts about God or feelings about God, and you are not imagining how God will be or should be. You are not involved in your image of God. You are simply aware of God.*

consider eternal life. Eternity and liberation exist only in the positive realms: Soul and above.

## Soul Realm

The Soul realm is the first level where the Soul is consciously aware of its own identity, its pure beingness, its oneness with God. As I have said, the Soul comes from and has its home in the Soul realm. In many ways, the Soul is a stranger to the lower realms, and there is always within it the thrust to return to its home, the realms of positive Spirit.

When we were born out of Spirit, we were born as a whole, complete Soul, and the Soul is perfect and made in the image of God. If the Soul is complete, whole, and perfect, why does it choose to incarnate? Because it is inexperienced. By coming into a physical body, it is gaining the experience of this level of God's creation.

Although the Soul is perfect and is our most important aspect, it is the weakest aspect in the physical world. The physical is by far the strongest, and on the physical level a person's astral, causal, mental, and etheric aspects are all stronger than the Soul. The Soul will allow these lower aspects to lead the consciousness because, no matter what happens, the Soul is gaining experience. The Soul does not

हू

*The Soul (which is who you are) is a small,
integral unit of energy, so beautiful that the
whole cosmos and all the universes are contained
within it. It is a prototype of all existence, complete in one energy unit. There is nothing that
exists anywhere in the universes of which you are
not a part, through the energy that is the Soul.*

interfere with this because it is a noninflictive energy, and it will not inflict against anything, including the false or lower self. Nor can it inflict against the false self or the Soul of anyone else. It is a paradox that the Soul is all-powerful, the spark of the Divine within, and on the physical level it is the weakest part of our makeup—until we find it. When we do find it, we can then learn to allow the Soul to lead us.

The noninflictive nature of the Soul also explains why people can spend whole lifetimes being unaware of the Soul's existence in themselves and in others and being caught up in the lower levels of their existence. Sometimes a person will feel a sadness and despair that nothing in this world can relieve. It is experienced almost as a feeling of homesickness, and that is actually what it is: they are sick of these lower levels, and they want to go home to the Soul realm.

Another paradox is that we do not have to go anywhere to be in the Soul. We are already there. We have only separated ourselves in consciousness from the Soul because of confusion through identification with our mind, our emotions, our body, and the material world. In the Soul, there is no separation. People have often asked me how I can know what is going on in a certain place. This is how: I step into the Soul, and in the Soul consciousness, my Soul

ध्रू

*The Soul's first name is Love, its middle name
is Truth, and its last name is Everlasting. Love
and Truth Everlasting.*

40

can communicate with any other Soul. It is instantaneous knowledge, faster than the speed of light. In the spiritual Light, everything is instantaneous and exists now. This is what people refer to as "the eternal now." It is when we come into the physical body that we come into space, time, differentiated energy, and various dimensions. Many people say, "I'm going to live for all eternity," and I say, "Yes, you are doing it right now. This *is* eternity." A thousand years from this point, if they say, "I'm going to live for eternity," the answer again will be, "Yes, you are."

I teach spiritual exercises, the most efficient and effective way I have found to move into the Soul. When you are moving in consciousness from the etheric realm to the Soul realm, you go through what is called the Rukmini Canal, a narrow opening between the two realms. It can be hard to find, but when you are working spiritually with the Mystical Traveler, the Traveler escorts you through and you do not have to consciously look for it or find it on your own.

Soul is another way of saying "I am." It is the highest level of consciousness available on the physical level. The Soul is intelligence: it just knows. In Hinduism it is called the *Atman,* a Sanskrit term meaning your essence, who you are. When you get to Soul, you can bring the Soul knowledge into the

द्यु

*There is so much there for you, once you open*
*yourself to it and begin to work consciously on*
*levels higher than that of Earth. It's all a mani-*
*festation of love. Love is the matrix that makes it*
*all possible. The energy of Spirit is the essence.*

physical, and you can correct the things in your life that need correction. You can make your life wonderful, beautiful, and joyous. You can learn how to manage on all the levels from Soul on down, moment by moment, decision by decision, knowing that consequences of your past actions will sometimes challenge you and that they can be experienced, handled, and released as they arise. It is possible to live your life in Soul consciousness right now in health, wealth, and happiness.

## Above the Soul Realm

There are twenty-seven distinct levels above the Soul realm. We call them the nameless realms, the inaccessible realms, the unavailable places; beyond that, there are no words for them, and you must experience them to know them. As I have said, the Soul realm is the first positive realm. When you go higher into the nameless realms of pure Spirit, it is neutral, neither positive nor negative, and Spirit is where everything originated.

In the beginning, there was Spirit. Spirit could not know Itself because It was all-pervasive. So out of Itself, It formed that which we call God. So then It became a Spirit God. But God in that form still could not know Itself because Spirit was all-pervasive. So then It formed Itself again out of Itself. But since that self was still Spirit, It still could not know Itself because It was still Spirit. As an analogy, my right hand cannot know my right hand because it has no reference point. But as I make another reference point (my left hand), I get to know my right hand.

But Spirit kept making Its "right hand" and could not know Itself. So then Spirit came down to Sat Nam (which means "true name"), which was the first extrusion of Spirit as an independent, whole-form God. Now Spirit could know Itself because It could see the God-form there in Sat Nam and the God-form in Itself. Sat Nam, the Lord of the Soul realm, became the Creator of all these universes.

## The Negative Power

The Lord of all the negative realms (those below the Soul realm) is called Kal Niranjan, also called Lucifer, Satan, or the devil in most Christian religions. We can also just refer to Kal as "the negative power." There is not a devil in the physical form, but there is definitely a negative energy, which permeates the planet. This negative energy manifests in thoughts and deeds of individuals and groups.

Kal sets up all the karma for the planet, which we all function under whether we like it or not, and the negative power functions out of the causal realm, since that is the realm of cause and effect. I call the negative power "the loyal forces of the opposition," since its job is to make sure we learn our lessons so that we can go back into the higher spiritual realms. It does much to strengthen us, and in this way it can be seen as positive.

In MSIA, we do not pay a lot of attention to the negative power, though we do learn how to hold a focus of loving in the face of it, because we keep our attention on where we are going—Soul Transcendence and God. We also do not talk much about the concepts of evil and hell, since good/God and heaven are where we are headed. In one sense, in fact, "heaven" could be seen as awareness of our oneness with God, and "hell" could be seen as forgetting our oneness with God. I look at evil as unnecessary experience. The Soul is here to gain experience, but not all experience is necessary. Some things are a detour, a distraction, yet since not one Soul will be lost, there is no unnecessary experience in the bigger picture. It just depends on how many millions of existences you want to have before you return home to God.

## Sounds, Colors, and Qualities of the Realms

When you are in the levels below Soul, primarily you are aware that you *see* the Light, and it is

# Chart of the Realms #2

| REALM | SOUND | COLOR |
|---|---|---|
| **POSITIVE REALMS** (Spirit) (Spiritual Light) | (Not verbalized) | (Not verbalized) |
| GOD | | |
| 27 Levels | HU | |
| | Woodwinds | |
| | Thousand violins | |
| | Angels singing | Clear |
| | Summer breeze through | Pale gold |
| | the willow trees | Light gold |
| SOUL | Haunting flutelike sound | Gold |
| **NEGATIVE REALMS** (Reembodiment levels) (Magnetic light) (Karmic Board) | *Cosmic Mirror* | |
| ETHERIC *(Unconscious)* | Buzzing bee or buzzing fly | Purple |
| MENTAL *(Mind)* | Running water or babbling brook | Blue |
| CAUSAL *(Emotions)* *(Karma)* | Tinkling bells | Orange |
| ASTRAL *(Imagination)* | Surf/waves | Pink |
| PHYSICAL *(Conscious self)* *(Physical body)* | Thunder; heartbeat | Green |

*Rukmini canal*

Subconscious
Unconscious
Habits
Addictions
Obsessions
Compulsions

(Note: High selves and basic selves may come from any level.)

beautiful. When you reach the Soul realm, you are part of the Light. You are *impressed* with the Light, which is actually the Sound Current, the audible Sound of God, which exists on all levels and can also be seen as various colors. In the Bible, the rod and staff are symbols of the Sound (the rod of power) and the Light (the staff that sustains all things).

For each realm, there is a particular color, sound, and quality. The colors are close to those listed on the Chart of the Realms #2, which also lists the sounds and qualities of each realm. The sounds given here are not exact but are an interpretation of sounds heard on the different realms, and the descriptive words are close enough to the actual sounds to give you something to listen for.

On the physical level, the sound may be like thunder. It is not a loud thunder, but it seems to be more of a steady sound. You might refer to it as a roar, something that just continues on, and it might seem unpleasant to you. It can also sound like a heartbeat. Sometimes there can be a loud popping sound. When you sense or hear this popping sound, it probably means that you have exteriorized part of your consciousness and that it is returning after having moved away from your body, which can happen during spiritual exercises and meditation.

On the astral realm, the sound is akin to the whoosh of ocean surf or the sound that you can hear when you hold a seashell to your ear. Sometimes you may feel this sound pulsating.

On the causal realm, the sound is tinkling bells, much like wind blowing through glass wind chimes. The bell sound can also be like the "bong" of a larger bell.

On the mental realm, it is the sound of moving water. It could be like a stream, a meandering brook, a waterfall, and even water being poured from a pitcher. The higher you go in the mental realm, the more refined the sound becomes so that it is almost like water running flat—and that does not make too much sound.

On the etheric realm, it is a buzzing sound, like that made by a bee, fly, or mosquito. This one can be very subtle, and you may have to listen extremely carefully to hear it.

In the Soul realm, there is a flutelike sound (it could sound like the flute you hear in an orchestra, a reed flute, or a piccolo), but it is not an ordinary flute. When that sound starts through your levels of consciousness, you are actually eating of spiritual food, the manna that comes from heaven. Once you hear this tone, you will never forget it. It is a haunting, almost drawing-to-you sound. It is not tugging because you will have no resistance; you *will* go to it. That is the sound referred to in the Bible: "In the beginning was the Word, and the Word was with God, and the Word was God" (John 1:1).

In the first realm above Soul, the sound is wind, the most delicate, tantalizing sound of a wind that you can imagine. It may sound like a breeze blowing through trees. If, in the wildest stretch of your imagination, you create what a beautiful wind sounds and feels like, you will still fall short of this sound.

Above that level, you will hear a humming sound, like the humming or singing of all the angels of all existences. It is not a loud or oppressive sound, yet you may feel as if it could rip you apart. At this point, you are moving into pure Spirit and dropping the identity of the Soul; every process and expression of individuality is being dropped.

Above that, the sound is of hundreds or thousands of violins. Very few people have ever gone this high and resided back in the physical body. Hearing that heavenly music can make this physical level extremely hard to live in.

Above this realm, the sound is like woodwinds: clarinets, oboes, saxophones, and flutes. The music is so perfectly divine that most people who reach that level want to stay there.

घु

*The Soul is positive in nature. The realm of the Soul and the realms of Spirit above the Soul are designed to lift us and bring us freedom. In the positive realms, the lower worlds lose their influence. The plan and purpose of the lower worlds become clear, and in that clarity is freedom.*

Eventually we get to the level of God, where the sound is Hu or H-U. In levels above this are the Silent Ones, but I am unable to give you any definition of this, and none of the sounds from these levels can be described in words or reproduced with the human voice. We in MSIA are working with a source of power that comes out of the Silence.

There are certain qualities associated with each realm. In the physical realm, one quality is *attention*. You need to be actively involved in your life and to pay attention to what is going on around you. At the same time, the challenge is not to get caught up in thinking that the physical level is the entire truth about yourself, for it actually represents only 10 percent of your existence, the other 90 percent being on the nonphysical realms. You also need the quality of *endurance* to work through and overcome any obstacles to your spiritual progression and to get up one more time than you fall.

On the astral realm, the challenge is to work with the quality of *ambition* and to apply it inwardly, to your spiritual growth. Your drive to succeed and accomplish can encourage you to check out the Traveler's teachings and see how they can assist you in moving towards Soul awareness.

धू

*At some point in your experiences and relation-*
*ships, you are going to come across a line into*
*the calm, quiet, and peacefulness of new expe-*
*rience. There is no emotion, there is no reference*
*point, there is just that which is. From there, you*
*can shift a step inward and start moving through*
*the spiritual worlds and find there worlds with-*
*out end. Where are you going? You say, "I'm*
*going to the Supreme God, to give myself over to*
*that." Then you say, "Put me where You want*
*me as part of You." At that moment, you will*
*have found your liberation.*

On the causal realm, *devotion* is the key to your spiritual progress. Your devotion is to who you really are, your Soul, and your devotion to doing spiritual exercises is the expression of the heartfelt yearning for greater awareness.

On the mental realm, the key is *dedication*. Combined with the devotional quality of the causal realm, dedication—to your true self and to your goal of Soul Transcendence—can be a powerful motivator.

When working in the etheric realm, *consecration* becomes the key. Each outward act and the inner act of doing spiritual exercises become consecrated to the Spirit within you.

The Soul realm is the realm on which true *liberation* is found. Not until you are awakened to your Soul will you find the freedom that is your joy and your heritage.

In the realms above Soul, the quality is *eternally traveling consciousness,* or ETC—with no period at the end. This is because there is always more. When you think that you have it, that you are there, that you know, go one step beyond that. Then go one step beyond that. No matter where you are and what you experience, do not stop there but keep going. Always, keep going.

ध्रू

*You can bring the spiritual essence into the
lower worlds and maintain it while you complete
your life here. The more you can move into the
Spirit as you live in this world, the more the
Kingdom of Heaven comes to hand. And the
more the Kingdom of Heaven comes to hand,
the more God reigns personally within you—as
both an inner and an outer form.*

## For More Information

*For an explanation of personal-use and public-use
MSIA materials, please see page 1.*

"Inner Journey Through Spirit Realms" (Public CD,
included with *When Are You Coming Home?*, hard-
bound book, ISBN: 978-1-893020-23-8). A beautiful
meditation through the realms into the "high
country" of your true self.

"The Sounds of the Realms" (Personal-use audio
seminar #2530). Basic information on the sounds of
each realm.

"The Hierarchy of Consciousness" (SAT #7114).
Explanation of your "court of influence," teachers
and guardian angels, and the masters above them.

*The Anointed One* (Personal-use CD set, ISBN: 978-1-
893020-39-9). The CD called "God-Traveler-Christ-
You" has information on the creation.

झू

## CHAPTER 3

# THE THREE SELVES

*The idea of the three selves encompasses many explanations for our consciousness. One psychologist said that when we are born, the mind is a* tabula rasa *(a blank slate). That is right; the conscious mind is a blank when we are born. Another said we have racial memory, like a group consciousness or great unconscious. That is right; that is the basic self. Others say that we have total knowledge and awareness. They are also right; that is the high self.*

## Overview

In the next chapter, I will go into detail about incarnation, which relates to one of the most fundamental questions of the human being: why am I here? Before I do that, I want to explain the three levels of consciousness that are part of our make-up:

the high self, the conscious self, and the basic self. An understanding of these will help you understand how incarnation works.

I am going to explain the idea of the three selves and give some examples. Especially if this information is new to you, you might approach it with openness and check out how it could apply to you and how you could use it for your growth and upliftment.

Here are brief descriptions of each:

The *conscious self* makes the conscious choices, gets up in the morning, drives the car to work, watches television, studies the reports, talks to friends, and so on. It is the part of you reading this book.

The *basic self* has responsibility for bodily functions, maintains habits and the psychic centers of the physical body, and handles prayers from the conscious to the high self. Much like a four- or five-year-old child, it tries to assert its desires and wishes upon the conscious self.

The *high self* functions as the spiritual guardian, directing the conscious self towards those experiences that will be for its greatest good. It has knowledge of the life destiny agreed upon before embodiment and attempts to fulfill it.

## The Conscious Self

The conscious self is the "captain of the ship" and can ignore or override both the basic self and the high self. This conscious aspect is the one most apt to get caught up in the illusions of the imagination, mind, and emotions and the glamour of the physical world, thus creating situations that may delay the Soul's evolvement. The conscious self usually functions out of the mouth, and to direct the conscious self, all we often need to do is keep the mouth shut.

When a human consciousness inflicts itself upon another human consciousness—when it creates harm, hurt, pain, etc., through physical action, thought patterns, verbal expressions, dishonesty, deceit, financial fraud, emotional control patterns, or any other way—it is held accountable for that and will be given the opportunity to clear the action and bring it into balance.

No one has the right to harm or hurt another in any way, and when that happens, the action must be balanced. It is the law of cause and effect: if you cause imbalance, the effect is that the imbalance is returned to you as its creator, and you get to make it right. This, in essence, is the action of karma. It is a just and fair action, and it is the creation of karmic

धू

*By chanting the initiation tone, you can move through the channels of your own subconscious, into the basic self. You can then thrust this tone (which is Sound and Light) up into your high self, and the high self gives back spiritual energy in return. Going through the basic self and up into the high self brings you into a oneness in all levels of your beingness. Energy patterns can then be reassembled, and new directions can be brought forward for you—out of your own conscious direction.*

situations that institutes the action of reincarnation. (Both karma and incarnation/reincarnation
will be explained in depth in later chapters.)

## The Basic Self

You may know there is another level within you
that you may have a hard time explaining in words
but that you can get very involved with. For example,
you might find yourself picking up something that
you do not want or need and putting it in your pock-
et. Why did you take it? Or you may "put your foot in
your mouth" or lose your temper and then wonder,
"Why on earth did I do that?" Many of these things
come from below the conscious level, which is the
level of the basic self. You could relate it to an animal
instinct or to the areas of memory, habits, or emotions. The basic self is all of these things and more.

The basic self will act primarily to preserve the
body. It will resist anything that will harm or hurt
the body or that will cause destruction to itself. As
an energy form, it is physically located in the stomach area. This can be the butterflies or knots in the
stomach, the hurt and depression. It can also be the
excitement, fun, and enthusiasm.

The basic self can be masculine or feminine, and
you can also have more than one basic self. For

example, a woman can have a female and/or male basic self, and the same is true for a man.

The term *inner child* has been in use recently, but this is not the same as the basic self. The inner child is more of a psychological description and is often used to refer to a person when they were a child. For example, people speak of "healing the inner child," which usually means healing memories of experiences a person had as a child.

## The High Self

The high self can be from any of the lower realms (astral, causal, mental, or etheric), and its physical location is usually about six to eight inches above the person's head. The high self can also be masculine or feminine. For the most part, the high self will act in the best interests of the Soul's progression and evolvement, and it will direct the human consciousness into those experiences it needs for its education.

The high self expresses the feelings of great inspiration and lofty ideals; it can create the desire in you to lift mankind in your arms and save everyone. Those moments when you see everything in the world in love, beauty, and harmony, those moments when everything is right and perfect, come out of the high self. Your will and the Father's will are one, but it is really that you are following the direction of your high self and fulfilling your destiny here on the planet.

## Working with the Three Selves

When a child is conceived, the basic self enters and starts making the child's body in the mother's womb. The high self, conscious self, and Soul hover around the mother, and the Soul and conscious self generally enter the child's body when the child takes its first breath. Both the basic self and high self still know the person's karmic plan at that time.

Then, when the child is around seven to eight years of age, the "veil of forgetfulness" for the basic self falls. From this point on, the basic self no longer has a complete working memory of the life plan, and the high self carries it. The plan is still with the basic but is dormant, and the basic depends on the conscious self to direct it. It can get upset, feel hurt, betrayed, let down, and confused or can bring dis-ease to the physical body if the conscious self does not communicate with it and direct it.

The relationship between the basic and conscious selves can be delicate. The basic can run things if the conscious self relinquishes responsibility. For example, the basic self can steal and make

ह्रू

*When you become the God-man, you have awareness on all levels simultaneously. You walk with your Beloved. You walk in a divine consciousness. What things look like down here doesn't really matter because you're in an attunement. You're walking with your high self, the Father-Mother God that resides above you as your extension into the one great Light.*

the conscious self feel guilty. Then if the conscious self represses this, this repressed energy can become a block between the high self and the conscious self. Because the high self is usually the communicator with Soul, the person may be blocking himself or herself from God.

The key thing to remember about the basic self is that it needs good, loving guidance. Have you ever walked around hand in hand with a little child? If you let go of them, they are kind of lost, and they come back and grab your hand. Basic selves function like that. They come back and grab your hand. They want to be more counseled, more guided, to have more direction. They want to be close and feel like you are there. If you do not do that with your basic self by giving it good, clean, clear direction, nurturing, and holding, it will start to look to somebody else for it. Then you may look at yourself and say, "I have a lousy life, I need a relationship," because your basic self is out looking around, but it cannot find anything because it does not have the ability to recognize it when it sees it.

Connect with the basic self. Keep talking to it, praising it, and loving it. If it does something wrong, you say, "That wasn't on target. Let's just do that once more." And the basic says, "Wow! Watch me, watch me!" and it hits the target. If you then say, "Well, you're *supposed* to hit the target," that is not what the basic wants. Instead, you say, "Wow! You hit the target! Great shot! And now we have to have more great shots." You give it a vision. But if you move off that first target to another one, you have to tell the basic self, "I'm going to move off that target to this other one." If you do not tell it—if you do not continually give the basic self clear direction—you will be moving someplace else, and it will still be back with the first one, and then both of them can get messed up.

The basic self loves to do and complete. So if you say you are going to do a certain thing (read a book, go back to school, balance your checkbook, travel in Europe, etc.) and then do not do it, the basic self still has energy tied up in that thing. So you need to say clearly and specifically that you are done with it if you are not going to do it. Broken agreements can be a big block between the conscious self and basic self and can undermine that relationship; then the basic may feel betrayed, confused, or let down, and you may not have all the support you need to accomplish things in your life. So be loving, clear, and responsible about what you say and do.

You want to come into alignment—basic self, conscious self, high self. And your purpose is spiritual:

how to get more of your Soul awareness functioning as you, instead of your ego functioning as you. This is something you discover just by living.

## Q&A About the Three Selves

**Q: Is there anything we can do to help a child when the veil of forgetfulness falls at around age seven?**

A: Maybe it's within the child's path that the memory veil falls, but at least you can keep the intellect aware that these other possibilities of awareness are still in existence, so that later on the person can make another choice to become aware of them again. Actually, what we are doing a great deal is going back and remembering when we were two, three, four, and five years of age.

**Q: Is the personality a combination of the basic self and conscious self?**

A: The personality is more a combination of the ego along with various karmic traits and inclinations that a Soul has agreed to bring into a lifetime.

**Q: Is there an esoteric meaning to "crossing" yourself, which is done in some churches?**

A: Years ago, when people would cross themselves, they would reach up to the high self, get

ह्यू

*As you keep moving towards the oneness, the wholeness of Spirit, you are reaching into the whole part of yourself where the basic self, conscious self, high self, and Soul are all perfectly aligned. When that occurs, you are awakened to the sacredness of your own being that has always been present and is present right now. You are all you will ever be. You are divine. You are perfection. All you have to do is awaken to that and then know it.*

hold of the spiritual power, bring it down with their hand to the basic self, come back up again to the heart center, and balance themselves out. When they would kiss the hand, this was to balance the action within them, to secure it within them.

## For More Information

*For an explanation of personal-use and public-use MSIA materials, please see page 1.*

"Knowing Your God Essence" (Public audio seminar #7391). Contains a loving demonstration of communication with the basic self.

"The Three Selves" (Personal-use audio seminar #1208). More information about the three levels of consciousness and how to work with them.

"So, Who's Taking Care of Whom?" (SAT #7035). How the three selves work together.

"What Is the Spiritual Marriage?" (SAT #7596). Information about the spiritual "marriage" of the high self, conscious self, and basic self.

# ध

## CHAPTER 4

# INCARNATION

*As long as a person identifies with anything other than his or her own beingness—the Soul—the person is in a state of incarnation.*

## A Soul's Journey

The concept of incarnation may be new to you. As a suggestion, you could read the information in this chapter and just remain neutral about it— neither disagreeing nor agreeing. It is what I have seen and experienced in the spiritual realms, and until you have the experience of these realms for yourself, you will not know for sure if it is really as I have described it. You could also entertain the possibility that the information is accurate and, if so, consider what that might imply to you in your life. No matter how you approach this, you are, as always, free to "take it or leave it."

The basic idea is that each of us is a divine Soul experiencing all of God's creation, which includes incarnating (embodying) on Earth. As a way of introducing an idea, here is a theoretical story of a Soul's experiences, told in very simplified, perhaps offbeat terms.

A Soul got bored one "day" and decided it would leave heaven, so it said to itself, "Thou art a rock." And sure enough, it was a rock. It found itself isolated (there weren't any other rocks around), and it couldn't move around very much. But this Soul was happy anyway because the nature of the Soul is joyful. The rock was heavier than anything else around it, so it kept sinking into denser areas until it came to the place called Earth. It settled down with a slight jolt and said, "Oh! I really am this rock." It didn't know what to do next, so it said, "I think I'll learn patience." It sat there for a long time, and in the course of thousands of years, the rock slowly eroded and broke apart.

The Soul said, "That's interesting. I'm freer now." But it wasn't really all that free because it had been absorbed into the land, and now it was being absorbed into a tree. That was a little better than being the rock; at least it could play in the sun and enjoy the breeze. It thought, "This is great. I'm really having a wonderful experience. I think I've learned patience being a rock. Now I think I'll learn gradualness."

So the Soul was part of the tree for a long time, until one day it decided to become the fruit on the tree. The fruit became ripe in its time, and it fell down and decayed. Then there appeared a worm that lived off the fruit, and soon the worm sprouted wings and discovered it could fly. The Soul said, "That's pretty good. I've learned patience and gradualness, and now I just have to learn elevation."

So the Soul flew around, and as it flew, a bird came along and absorbed it. The Soul said, "This is fine. Now I'm bigger and can fly higher." But before long, an animal came along and consumed the bird. The animal couldn't fly, but it could run very fast, so the Soul said, "I think I'll learn mobility on the earth."

The Soul discovered that the new form was strong, and it lived a long time in this form. Eventually, though, the form passed from the earth, and the Soul discovered itself in a new form, that of a human being. And through many lifetimes in human form, the Soul discovered that it had greater freedom than ever. It realized the reality of itself. It realized that it had always been a Soul and that it had had all these other experiences but had

घू

*When God awakened and moved upon Himself and breathed forward all the worlds, He did it for Himself, which is within each Soul. He did it for each one of us to come into this experience and have happiness and joy beyond all imagining.*

never really been any of them. It had always been just what it was: a Soul, a part of God.

It also discovered that the strength of the Soul is far greater than the physical strength of the beast, and it found that its beingness is far more magnificent than the most magnificent earthly monarch. It discovered that its kingdom is neither on nor of the earth. So after many lifetimes, it said, "I don't belong here," and it just dropped that physical form and moved directly into the Soul realm, its home, where it was greeted regally. It entered royally and sat on the throne because it was the king of its own principality.

The reality of a Soul's evolvement is more complex, of course; perhaps this story conveys the essence of it.

## Why Do Souls Incarnate?

In the beginning of time, God was in all places in an absolutely pure state, and in this purity, It was a void, without specific consciousness. God did not know Itself in Its greater beingness, so God instituted patterns of creation. It created universes, within which were what appeared to be solid objects (which we call planets) and less solid material (which we call space). All of it is God in God's different manifestations. God also instituted the plan that every part

ध्रु

*Before you came into embodiment, you intended to become more aware and to use this level to bring yourself into God consciousness, to leave this land of reflected Light and enter into the ultimate, and then to take the next step as it is presented to you, for you.*

would know every other part, through experience. Thus the Soul, which is more directly the spark of God, was evolved and was given the opportunity to experience all levels, layers, planes, and realms of experience and being.

Soul can inhabit any form it wishes. Its reason for being, its "job," is to experience all it can on every level it can, thereby growing in awareness of its own divine nature. And the Soul that has experienced all is God, is one with God. But this experience of God is tremendously large and complex, so the Soul spends enormous amounts of time in its evolvement through the realms of experience back into the awareness and knowledge of its divine nature.

## Incarnation in the Lower Realms

To recap the information in chapter 2, The Realms of Spirit, there are the lower (or "negative") realms, the positive realms of Spirit starting with the Soul realm, and the neutral, nameless realms of Spirit above those. The Soul has its home in the Soul realm and, in many ways, is a stranger to the lower realms; within the Soul is always the thrust to return to the realms of positive Spirit and above.

The Soul incarnates in the lower realms to gain the experience of those parts of God. It may incarnate

ध्रू

*The earth is one of those places where the Soul*
*can get the most experience in the shortest period*
*of time, so it chooses to come here as often as is*
*necessary for the correct and useful experiences*
*and to clean up incompletes from past existences.*
*The Soul needs these experiences so it will know*
*how to be an effective and efficient creator.*

in any of the lower realms, and it picks up the body (sheath) of the realm on which it incarnates. Each form is heavier and denser than the one before, and the physical form (physical body) is the densest.

The physical realm is unique in that when a Soul incarnates on this level, it also has levels of consciousness that reflect the other lower realms: unconscious, mind, emotions, and imagination. As the Soul takes on these different aspects, which are all reflections of the negative realms, it remains as the one positive aspect among all the negative aspects. (And, again, "negative" does not mean "bad.") The Soul becomes the weakest part in the physical form because its job is to experience the lower realms through the physical form. This is what you, as the Soul that you truly are, are doing here on Earth: gaining experience.

## Why Do We Come Here So Many Times?

As a human, a Soul starts by incarnating once onto the physical realm, into a physical form; any future times it comes here are more accurately called embodiments. If that first form could walk through its life here in perfect balance, creating only peace, love, and harmony, it might complete and free itself from this realm and earn the opportunity to continue

ॠ

*This earth experience is valuable for you because it is the garbage dump, and out of garbage you get compost, out of the compost you get fertility, out of fertility you get life, out of life you get awareness, out of awareness you get Soul recognition, out of Soul recognition you are recognized by Spirit, and in that recognition you become a co-creator with God.*

its evolvement on higher realms. But when the Soul incarnates into a physical form, it is usually inexperienced in the ways of this world. The consciousness sees all the glamour, illusions, attractions, and pleasures of the world, and it gets sidetracked. But even though the Soul gets pulled into these things, they are all a part of its learning.

As the Soul goes through its life plan, it is apt to create imbalance. Then when the time comes for the physical body to die, there are often karmic situations that have not yet been cleared or balanced. Thus, the Soul, at a later time, embodies again onto the physical realm so that it can clear its debts, right the wrongs, and bring balance and harmony. But if the consciousness again gets caught up in the illusions and the glamour, it may end up creating more karmic situations so that the Soul must again embody to clear them. And so on. (Karma is explained at length in the next chapter, Karma: Creation and Fulfillment.)

At some point, the consciousness will come into an understanding of this whole process; it will learn to be a responsible creator and to place its value and its concern on those things that are positive and spiritual in nature rather than on the materiality of this world. In this way, the consciousness begins its evolution back towards God, fulfills its karma from the past, stays free of accruing more karma, and liberates itself from this world. It is everyone's heritage—it is your heritage—to know the divine nature, to experience the joy, freedom, and perfection of the Soul.

## Female and Male Polarity

The Soul, in itself, is both positive and negative and is complete in its energy pattern. But when it decides to come into a physical form, it orients itself more towards one or the other polarity—female or male. It may say, "I'm going to come onto the earth this time as a male." So the high self, which works with the Soul, will go to the repository of basic selves and get a basic self that will be able to bring a body into the correct form for this incarnation, and the basic self will begin to form the male body during gestation.

Although the Soul will embody into the form as a male expression at the time of birth, its energy is still complete within itself because the Soul is perfect and complete, beyond gender. But the polarity of the *body* may feel the need for the balance of the opposite polarity, and so it will seek a mate, a companion, someone with whom it can exchange energy and feel complete.

The male form expresses primarily a positive polarity; the female expresses primarily a negative polarity. These polarities are neither good nor bad but are like the negative and positive poles of a battery. When male and female polarities come together in the sexual encounter, the energies are exchanged; in essence, the "battery" is charged.

When you recognize that the Soul is perfect and complete, you have found your "Soul mate." The *Soul* does not look for a mate because it is perfect. It is the lower levels of consciousness that look for a mate, that seek to complete themselves. When you recognize that you are complete, then you will have no need for the boundaries of this world, and this is what is often called self-realization. It is freedom.

**When Were Souls Created?**

All Souls were created at one "time." Souls have always been, but they have chosen different occasions to incarnate on this planet and gain their experiences. So each Soul is not equal in its progression and development, even though all are equal in the higher reality. Also, the time patterns between embodiments may vary, and there is no average time between embodiments. So, although all Souls were created simultaneously, one may have experienced

ह्रू

*Because the Soul has little concern about time or space, it is unconcerned with the trials of the physical, emotional, or mental levels. It moves into the physical body, inhabits it, and has a wonderful time doing the divine dance of God. In the midst of your personality trivialities, the Soul is laughing.*

more than another. One person may be experiencing his or her fiftieth lifetime here while another may be experiencing the hundred and ninety-fifth. That will make a considerable difference in each one's awareness of Spirit and in each one's expression.

## Races on the Earth

Over the eons of time on the planet, there have been many races of people. Right now, the white race is the dominant race ("dominant" does not mean "better"), but this has not always been the case. Each race is a different experience, a different consciousness. It is all one spiritually, but there is a separate consciousness within each race. You may not acquire the experience to know all of God in all Its dominion unless you incarnate through all cycles. You may reembody as a red person one lifetime and learn it and never need to come back into that consciousness, or you may come in one lifetime as a black, brown, white, or yellow person and learn it and never need to come back in that consciousness. It would be rare, however, to complete those experiences in one lifetime. When you get down here on the planet in all the levels of karmic fulfillment, it becomes difficult to fulfill all conditions in one lifetime.

घू

*If you want release from incarnation patterns, start assuming responsibility immediately, in this moment.*

## Your Decisions Before Incarnation

As I said in the previous chapter, before you—the Soul—incarnate on the planet, you are in consciousness on some other realm; you are living another existence. But, for whatever reason, it becomes time for you to incarnate on the physical realm. Keep in mind that it is the nature of the Soul to experience all levels and conditions of God. Thus, the earth experience is part of the Soul's evolution into the greater consciousness of God.

Before you incarnate or reembody, you (as the Soul) meet with the high self and the Karmic Board, karmic counselors or masters who have access to the Akashic Records, where everything you (the Soul) have ever done is recorded. You all meet to plan your life on the planet within high degrees of possibility and probability. At this time of planning, you choose such things as your parents, the talents and abilities you will have, the challenges and situations you need to face, and so on. You choose those things that you and the karmic counselors decide will be best for you to further your spiritual progression. And that is a big key to understanding this life: you choose it all. You also set up the situations that will bring you together with people in relationships that will give you the opportunity to fulfill karmic debts from your past existences. Then a basic self is chosen that can carry out this pattern.

All this is usually done many years ahead of your incarnation unless you are on a "speed-up" plan. It is interesting that a lot of the young people who were in the "hippie" movement in the 1960s were in World War II. They resented that war very much, and they were not about to go into a war again. They would tell you about war and the horrors of it because it was fresh in their conscious memory.

## Conception, Gestation, and Birth

Within twenty-four hours after conception, the basic self will come in and start making the body of the child in the mother's womb, pulling together the essences from the chromosomes and genetic formation. Though it may seem to be random choice, it really is not; it is done through the spiritual essence. The chromosomes are brought together in the correct way, based on all the karmic paths physically, mentally, emotionally, spiritually, sexually, financially, and so on. It is all written through here.

During gestation, as early as from a month or two, but usually around the seventh month of pregnancy, the Soul, high self, and conscious self will hover around the mother, and she may feel their presence with her. During this time, however, the basic self has total jurisdiction over the body of the fetus. It can abort the fetus or cause a miscarriage if it feels incompatible, if, for example, some newly created condition by the parents (particularly the mother) alters the original plan. If the basic self is to have the experience just through gestation, the baby can be stillborn.

At the time the body comes into the world, the Soul breathes into it, and the Soul and the conscious self enter the body. The first breath of life is infused with what we call the Soul. This is the divine spark that comes into this temporal image that we are going to walk around with. At that point, the high self will usually anchor right nearby, hovering around the body.

The Soul usually comes into the body at birth, though it will sometimes come in only partly and hover nearby. In some cases, it might not come into the body until it is six or seven years of age. But it would be nearby, and the basic self would be handling the things of the body and doing all the things that are necessary.

ध्रू

As you begin the inner journey, you will find
that you are the only one who can decide what is
right for you. You become responsible for yourself and to yourself, and to no others.

## Free Will and Free Choice

You might say, "Well, I don't have much choice, do I?" Before incarnation you have *free will* and you exercise it; after you incarnate, you have *free choice*. Before you incarnate, you freely set up many possibilities; after you incarnate, you choose which of the possibilities you wish to follow. You are making all your choices before you come in, and then you unfold them. You discover as you go along what the path is. But there are a lot of alternate choices if you get off the path, and before you incarnated, you saw ahead to those choices, too.

It is very complex and complicated to lay out all the variables that you can possibly enter into in your lifetime, so complex that a computer would probably be inadequate to do what can be done by the masters of the Karmic Board who know, down to the most minute detail, what has happened through all of your existences. They sit with you, and then they sit with the Souls of your potential parents and family, and these patterns of your existence are worked out through many generations.

Here is an example of how this could work: within your karmic pattern, the counselors may set up actions whereby you work with the pattern of patience. In a former situation, you may have been very impatient with people and cut them off short, possibly by way of their heads. Because you created this action, you are going to have to enter into situations where you will not necessarily lose your head physically, but you will be experiencing impatience and "losing your head" in other ways, maybe through emotions or temper. The action may be symbolic rather than physical. You will enter into these situations to learn to become patient.

It may be set up so that the one person who keys off this impatience pattern for you is someone from a previous lifetime who was a receiver of your action. Perhaps, for example, he will be your father this time. Before you embody, you agree to the action and the conditions because it is fair that he gets the chance to balance the action. In situations of this sort, it is even possible that when the child incarnates, the father will see the child and experience a recall (not often on the conscious level) of the past life and kill the child. This has happened, although it usually does not happen because the father will generally give the child the opportunity to balance and fulfill the action.

These opportunities are so perfect. If you ever do something that is inflicting on another and play the little mental game of, "Oh, nobody knows; I can get away with it," think again. You are not getting away with anything. The Soul records it all and holds itself responsible for it all, in perfection, justice, and great love.

## Past Lives

The basic reason people usually do not remember their past lives is lack of awareness. Also, when human beings leave the body—die from the physical plane—they often do so in situations that are fearful for one reason or another. Their cry, at the moment of death, may have been, "Oh, God, I don't want to die. *I don't want to die!*" And they have hung on to the physical body and died terror-stricken. If they were later to have knowledge of their past lives, they would also have knowledge of their past deaths that were unpleasant and fearful, and, as human beings, we will attempt to conceal the trauma, so we block the memories.

Psychiatry, psychology, primal therapy, deep-massage techniques, and so on are all designed to get at the old traumas and release them. They are "screaming" the cell levels loose. But it does not have to be done that way. All you really have to do is start living *now,* start taking care of *now,* and let the past traumas drop away. It can be done that way, and your attitude is the key. If you think that screaming will

ध्रु

*The key to breaking free is to love yourself and to love each experience that comes to you, whether it appears to be negative or positive. Love it all equally.*

release the past trauma, then there is a good chance that it will. But if you think that just blessing the past with love and focusing all your energies on the *now* will release the traumas, then there is a good chance that it will work.

I rarely tell people about their past lives because the specifics really do not matter all that much to you in this life. What matters much more is that you focus on *now* and on taking care of what is up in your life *now*. When you do that, the past—of this life and of former existences—gets handled as well.

Another reason I usually do not comment on past lives is that if a person knows about a past life, they can sometimes hang on to it, perhaps because they romanticize it, judge it and what they did in it, or think it gives them an excuse for why things are as they are in their current life. Their consciousness can get trapped in that past existence, but it is *past*. It is not a very useful way to live, either physically or spiritually.

## Ending the Incarnation Cycle

Reincarnation is not negative, as a lot of people would like to believe. It is a very positive, progressive philosophy: if you don't make it now, you get another chance. What could be better than that? Still,

धू

*It takes great courage to see the face of God.
The face of God lies on the other side of all the
illusions of the physical, imaginative, emotional, mental, and unconscious worlds. The way to
the other side is through all of that. With the
grace of the Traveler, you can tap into the consciousness of the Soul and use that higher perspective to guide your way so that you do not get
trapped once again in the highways and byways
of the lower worlds.*

though, MSIA does not teach reincarnation. We teach
Soul Transcendence and getting off the planet.

Everyone, whether they realize it or not, is
working for awareness of the inner consciousness,
seeking first the Kingdom of God within and then
seeking God in the outer reality. And everybody
wants to reach heaven. But if you were told you
were going to die in two weeks, you would probably
say, "Oh, God, no. I don't want to die. I want to stay
in this misery." And with that attitude you will,
either now or later. You must be extremely careful
about how you place things towards yourself because,
being a creator and having the divine essence within
you, you will be held responsible, and that which
you create will be returned to you.

It is natural for the Soul to incarnate onto the
physical plane to gain experience, but it is the action
of karma—the creation and the releasing of karma—
that perpetuates the action of reembodiment. Many
people have lived hundreds of lives on Earth and are
still attempting to gain an understanding of karma
so they can release themselves from the cycle of
incarnation, realize the freedom of their Soul, transcend this realm, and know the higher realms.
Through the teachings of the Movement of Spiritual
Inner Awareness, you can end the incarnation cycle.

घू

*These lower levels can be full of errors, frustrations, and mistakes. They're designed that way. They're designed to refine your level of awareness so you can discover more completely who you are.*

## Q&A About Incarnation

**Q: If we have a Soul inside of us that is perfect and if we started off perfect before we came here to this planet, why do we have to go through this "hell," so that we can go through these experiences, so that we can progress, so that we can go back and be perfect?**

A: The Soul's being perfect does not equate to the Soul's being experienced. If being here were based upon the Soul's perfection, then the Soul would not be here to start with. But the Soul's job is to gain experience, and one of the ways it can do that is by coming here. The Soul is to gain experience and to become a co-creator with God. Perfection does not necessarily know how to create. It is a *being* state. It also does not necessarily know right-wrong configurations; it sees these situations only as a perfection in the whole.

**Q: Some people talk about getting off the wheel of 84 when they mean they want to stop incarnating. What is "the wheel of 84"?**

A: A *lakh* is 1,000 years. In ancient Indian religions, it was said that it took 84 *lakhs* (or 84,000 years) to progress into God consciousness. Hence, "the wheel of 84."

Q: When you talk about "making it," does this mean the Soul gets off the planet, and the basic self, conscious self, and high self still come back?

A: When we talk about making it off the planet, we're talking about the Soul's having gained its experiences and not needing to incarnate here again. The high self and the basic self go to the repositories for high selves and basic selves, and they hold there until they are called forward again to fulfill a certain karmic plan for another Soul. Then they are drawn forward again with all the "positive" and "negative" attributes, as we would term them; within themselves, however, all attributes are positive.

Q: What happens in the repository for basic selves?

A: When the basic self leaves a physical body and goes back to the repository of basic selves, it goes through a cleansing action. And then it is refortified to the jobs of the basic self.

When a basic self learns its lessons, it can then move into being a conscious self and then into being a high self. All its positive attributes move into the Soul. Eventually, all positive attributes will be here, and they will be in the Soul consciousness. The Soul then has great experience.

Q: The conscious self that I have now—was it somebody else's conscious self in another lifetime?

A: It could have been but might not have been. Some people incarnate all the way right through their own birth pattern, like they are their own great-great-great-great-great-great-grandfather, and they just keep incarnating back in their own line. That's not unusual at all. We find this especially with Oriental people because of their reverence for ancestors. It is where they place their consciousness, and they may continually incarnate back in the same line.

Q: When you reembody, do you always come in with the same basic self and high self?

A: No, it would be a waste of time to come in with the same ones. You come in with diverse basic and high selves, in order that the Soul can experience more things.

Q: Why is there such a focus in the MSIA teachings on getting off the planet when we would not be here if this planet were not our perfect learning ground?

A: The planet *is* the perfect learning ground, and there are much nicer places to be than this planet. After the lessons of this planet are learned, the Soul

ह्रू

*Life really is just humor at its funniest state.*
*Sometimes it gets so funny you can even laugh.*
*And there is no need to substitute crying for*
*laughing.*

then goes to other realms of consciousness. Ultimately, a Soul will know itself fully as being one with the Supreme God, and the Soul's final state is to become a co-creator in the oneness of it all. Rarely does that occur when a person is in a physical body.

**Q: I have the sense that I didn't want to be here in a physical body or wasn't ready and that I hold a grudge towards God because I'm here.**

A: When a Soul incarnates here, it is because the Soul decided to do this beforehand, in the Spirit world. On the spiritual levels, this decision often looks easy—like, "of course"—and it can look hard or dumb from the limited perspective of this physical planet.

There can also be a memory of the clarity and connection that's in the Spirit, and if it is not as evident to the consciousness, anger can be turned towards God. The anger is misplaced, however, since it was the Soul itself that freely made the decision to come here. The anger can usually be resolved when the misunderstandings are released and forgiven.

**Q: If we do have to reembody, when will we reach the point at which we can be with God without separating from Him in any way?**

A: It happens at any time in Spirit.

ध्रू

*If you stay within the teachings and the consciousness of the Traveler, you can be free of the cycle of return this lifetime. Everyone will get off this cycle eventually. Everyone will make it. Don't worry about it; don't be concerned. Spirit is not worried. Your Soul is not worried. It knows the perfection. It sees it already accomplished. All you have to do is walk the body and the consciousness through the steps of the process.*

Q: Can any one individual Soul return to God when it is ready, or do we all have to wait until all Souls are ready, so all Souls return together? If we are all one, can any individual return without the others returning as well?

A: An individual Soul can return to God when it is ready, but the whole (rather gigantic) action won't be complete until all Souls return to God. The Soul has no problem with this. Its perspective is that it is getting experiences, and it does not perceive itself as separate from God, so there is not the anguish of separation that the personality and ego can sometimes feel.

Q: What is the Soul, and what is Spirit?

A: Soul is eternal throughout all of existence. Spirit is the essence that pervades.

Q: Then what is the difference between God and Spirit?

A: As an analogy, Spirit is everything in a room you *can't* see, and God is everything in the room you *can* see. There is a difference. Everything that is manifested (that which we can see) comes from that which we cannot see.

The great invisible Spirit God issued forth God as a first-form manifestation for these creations. So

ह्रू

*Anyone who is residing in the power of love is never destroyed, never separated, always free, always up, always growing.*

what you actually have is God in a huge extension that comes down and finally shows Itself.

**Q: So I am an extension of God.**

A: Absolutely. Unquestionably, that is so. But you're like the small drop in the ocean compared to all the other drops in the ocean, so you can't do an ego trip. But, still, you are part of it, and every part makes up the whole.

That's why not one Soul will be lost—because God reclaims all of Itself to Itself. But since It only deals in creativity, not in time, there are no time elements on us. It is when we feel the yearning of the Soul that we turn towards God and start to move our journey that way. Once the Soul separates from the mind, we see the effulgent beauty of our whole beingness, and we're homesick until we rush into the very center of God. At that point, depending upon our experiences, either we lose identification or we retain identity and become a Lord God Creator over the dimensions.

घृ

*Your job is to experience. That's all you have to do. It is in the* loving *of your experience, the* loving *of your expression, that you discover the inner joy, the bliss that is your indication of the presence of the Traveler.*

## For More Information

*For an explanation of personal-use and public-use MSIA materials, please see page 1.*

"States of Evolvement" (Personal-use audio seminar #2567). Learning on the planet and evolving into Spirit.

*The Journey of a Soul* (Paperbound book, ISBN: 978-1-893020-13-9). Information on incarnation. Much of the material in this chapter comes from this early book by J-R.

ध

## CHAPTER 5

# KARMA: CREATION AND FULFILLMENT

*The law of karma, taken beyond the context of a single life, is the foundation for reincarnation. Often, the imbalances that you have created in your life through abuse and misuse of many aspects of your consciousness cannot be balanced in one lifetime. So the consciousness returns to this physical level to fulfill the debts incurred and balance the action. The law of karma is a just and perfect system and ensures that those who evolve into Soul consciousness have a deep and true knowledge of all levels of consciousness.*

Human beings are an extension of God and, as such, they have certain attributes in common with God. One is the power of creation. Part of our experience on the physical plane is to become a consciously aware and responsible creator and to create those things which are positive in nature. We create by our emotions, thoughts, words, and actions. We can create misery, hurt, fear, revenge, etc., or we can create happiness, harmony, confidence, peace, and joy. And each of us makes these choices many times each day.

## How Do We Create Karma?

Karma is the law of cause and effect: as you sow, so you reap. Simply stated, what you put out, you get back. People usually use the word *karma* to refer to something that is difficult or upsetting, but there is also good karma. It is good karma, for example, for a person to study spiritually with the Mystical Traveler. For now, though, I will talk about karma as an imbalance from one time that still needs to be cleared or balanced.

There is often a comparatively large time gap between the instigation of an action and its result, between the cause and the effect. This is one reason it is difficult for people to recognize the relationship between the cause and the effect. If you steal a car and go joy-riding when you are sixteen, and twenty years later a bunch of kids steal your brand-new Cadillac and wreck it, it may be difficult for you to see the connection. But it is there. It is just your action being returned to you.

This also applies from one existence to another existence. When you consider that your Soul has probably had many, many physical and nonphysical existences prior to this one, you can probably imagine that there would be quite a bit of karma that would need to be cleared and that the time lag between the cause and the effect may be lost in the mists of time. But it is safe for you to assume that almost everything you have in this lifetime is connected in some way to your experiences in past existences. Sometimes the connection is big and obvious, and other times, it is subtle. But it really does not matter a whole lot if something is "karmic" or not because you still need to handle the situation in this life.

Karma can be created in several ways and through seemingly infinite situations. Basically, karma is accrued by transgressing your own consciousness or the divine consciousness in another person. Any action, emotion, thought, or word that is put forth in an out-of-balance way may cause karma. For example, if you become angry and strike your child, that may very well create a karmic situation. Later you may apologize, which clears the karmic action. But if the child has done something it should not do, "spanking" may be the way that you make the child become aware of and understand its error.

घू

*Don't be shocked at or condemn yourself over
how unaware you've been for years. When the
veil is parted and you see spiritually, you may
see many of the imbalances you've created. As
a result, you could enter into condemnation
unless you keep the spiritual door open and continually receive the flow of grace, the divine
consciousness. When you can do that, you may
clear all those past imbalances.*

(I am not talking about *beating* the child.) And if you spank the child in love and discipline, not out of anger, you have created no karma, nor will you feel it necessary to apologize. You are merely helping the child to learn. Attitude, as this example shows, can make a big difference in whether or not you create karma.

You can bring many karmic situations to yourself through misuse of your emotional nature. (You might think that if this is so, you will have karma the rest of your life. You may, but you will be a day older whether you work to clear your karma or not, so you might as well work on it.) If you feel anger, if you feel hate, if you desire revenge, if you feel guilt or any of the other negative emotions, you bring karma to yourself. If you bring it in and hold on to it, you will be held accountable for it.

The Soul is perfect; the personality is imperfect. But since the Soul has contracted to experience the physical realm with a particular personality and consciousness, it will reembody to fulfill the karmic situations accrued by the personality. The personality usually brings about karma through overindulgence. When you get so angry that you are out of control, when you continually get so emotionally upset that you cannot control your tears and your

धू

*Don't sit in judgment of your own lack of awareness or anyone else's. The action of judging demonstrates lack of awareness.*

sobs, when you get so drunk that you cannot remember or control what you do, when you get so "spaced out" on drugs that you are not in control—these situations bring karma to you. And, probably more than any other single thing, the guilt you feel after these overindulgences will bring karma to you.

If you cheat on your spouse, that may bring a karmic situation, but it might be relatively easy to clear and balance. But if you also feel guilty about this, you can lock that karma to yourself for a lifetime or longer. If you have a child and give that child up for adoption, that may be a clear action, and you may accrue no karma from doing it. But if you feel that you should not have done it—if you feel guilty—you can make it a karmic situation. If you become pregnant and decide to have an abortion, that decision and situation may be free of karma. But if you feel guilt and remorse and beat yourself up emotionally and mentally because of the action, you can produce a karmic situation. It is very much a question of attitude.

There are many, many experiences on this realm. Most of them are not inherently "good" or "bad," but the attitude with which they are carried out may very well create a value judgment, which, if the judgment is "bad," may create guilt, and that, in turn, will create karma. In fact, the biggest thing that builds karma is guilt. If we do something and we have a second thought—"I wonder if I should have done that"—we have karma. It is important to watch the attitude and keep it as neutral as possible. (See chapter 18, The Importance of Attitude, for more on this.)

## Balancing Karma

The idea of creating and fulfilling karma is incredibly complex. There are many, many planes and levels on which to create and fulfill karma. If you multiply all of those by all of the situations, relationships, and attitudes that can create and fulfill karma, you have what appear to be infinite possibilities. And you have to learn to recognize—and then bypass—every one.

Many times, karmic situations are both created and fulfilled in one lifetime. Say, for example, that a man marries a woman with whom he is very much in love. He thinks she is the greatest woman in the world, gives her everything, and treats her like a princess, and then he finds out that she is unfaithful to him. Her unfaithfulness causes him tremendous anguish and pain, and the marriage eventually ends in divorce. Several years later, she marries again. She is very much in love with her new husband and thinks he is the greatest guy in the world, and then she finds out after a while that he is being unfaithful to her. She is getting the opportunity to experience what she caused to be experienced. In the first marriage she was the cause; in the second, the effect. Really, though it might not seem so, she is lucky because she is getting to balance the karma this lifetime. If it was not balanced this time, it would be balanced during another lifetime because nothing is overlooked.

As another example, if, through deceit and lies, you caused someone to go to jail unjustly, you may find yourself at some future point imprisoned for a crime that you did not commit. If you then accept what is happening and learn all you can from the experience, you will balance and clear the karmic debt. But if you go into hate, anger, and revenge, you will perpetuate your karma and get to experience it again and again until you learn to bring yourself into balance with it. You might not experience imprisonment as a physical prison experience, but perhaps you might find yourself "trapped" in a job you cannot stand and unable, for some reason, to change that situation. You might find yourself "trapped" in a family situation or in a marriage. There are a lot of ways to be imprisoned.

घू

*When something happens that appears to hurt you, rather than resisting it and pushing it away, you will embrace it. You will expand your consciousness to encompass the changes and the new situation and to find what new freedoms are available to you.*

When you begin to understand karma, you can begin to realize that some actions that appear to be "bad" may be actions of fulfilling karma and, therefore, right and proper within that framework. For example, in a previous lifetime, a mother abandons her child and leaves it in the hands of people who do not really care for the child. Because the mother refused to accept and handle her responsibility for the child, the child grew up unloved, abused, misused, and leading a very unhappy, embittered life. The child reembodies at some point, grows up, and has a child of her own, who happens to be her mother from the previous life. She may feel no love for her baby and may abandon it, giving it the opportunity to have the same experience and learn what it is like to be abandoned and unloved. People who observe this might be apt to judge this mother for abandoning the child, when she is actually only fulfilling the karma and bringing to the other consciousness the experience that is necessary to free it from the karma it had created in that other lifetime. So unless you can read the karmic records and see what is within each person's heart, it is best not to judge actions that appear to be unusual or cruel. It may be an action fulfilling a karmic debt.

Let's look at another situation. Suppose one of the karmic things that you have brought forward to work out is getting too emotionally involved with your loved one. When you love someone (let's say it is a man), you may want to breathe his air for him, help him digest his food, and make sure that his heart beats just right and that the blood circulates in just the right places. You often see this type of love in the love of mothers and fathers for their children. They want everything to be so perfect for their children that they try to protect them from life itself, but it cannot be done. As much as you love people and try to bring their lives under your control, it just cannot be done.

If you feel that someone is not living their life the way you would like them to, you can feel hurt and rejected and can start going into emotional patterns. You do not intellectualize; you may think you do, but you do not. You then add emotions to the thoughts. You mess up your thinking and circle your thoughts around. You send out thoughts of hurt, frustration, and bitterness, and it becomes self-pity time: "Woe is me. I feel so sorry for me. They don't understand. They hurt me. They don't do what I want them to do, what I need them to do."

These thoughts come out emotionally charged, and then they come right back around and hit you in the stomach. You will often feel your energy drain off as you feel this rejection. You may push the feeling of rejection down to the creative center, and then when your loved one wants to come close and make love with you, you say, "No way! Now, how do you like feeling rejected?" So you deny them and produce a karmic situation. But the karmic situation is produced from the dishonesty and the deceit accompanying the action, not necessarily by the action itself. An honest approach would be to say, "Look, today you said something that hurt my feelings, and I really felt rejected and upset. So it is going to be very difficult for me to make love with you and feel good about it."

Your partner will probably say, "Wow, what did I say that hurt your feelings?"

You might say, "It was that comment about me being overweight."

And your partner may say, "Honey, I was just kidding. I was teasing. I didn't mean anything. But, you know, I've been putting on some weight lately, so maybe we could both start watching our diet a little more." This is being honest and communicating. This is clearing the air.

These things are very important. Most of our karmas deal with communication one way or another—too much or too little. If you communicate honestly and keep the air clear between you and the people you live and work with, you will probably be staying pretty free of accruing karma. It is when you let the little hurts, resentments, injustices, and irritations build up that you are creating karma.

## Sharing Karma

Many times people come together in a marriage or in a family to help one another work through karmic situations, but you actually have karma only with yourself, not necessarily with other people. Other people usually come into the situation only to give you the opportunity to handle your own karma; they fit within your karmic flow. If they flow into it the way you like it, you call that "good karma." If they fit into it in ways that you do not like, you call it "bad karma." But the karma is not actually good or bad. The karma just is.

In family situations, karma can become so involved that we often say families share karma. For example, a young man and woman may get married in a situation where she has (before their marriage) run up large bills at various department stores around town. Before the marriage, the man is not connected to that action in any way at all. After the marriage, he is responsible for those debts. He shares her financial karma, and the law may hold him liable for payment. That is an obvious example, and most are far more subtle.

If you get married, almost 100 percent of the karma is affected, and you can take on the karma of your spouse. If you are almost free of karma and you get a spouse who is loaded with it, then you have said that "we are one," and you get it. Then if the child that comes through you happens to be a real "whoop-de-do," you have quite a household going. So what does this tell you? That you cannot go on stupidly blundering through your life. If you are going to get married, marry somebody who is pretty close to your same evolvement.

Many people seem to have relatively few problems before marriage, but when they get married they seem to have quite a lot of problems and difficult situations for a while. Then everything settles down and seems all right again. It takes time for both partners to adjust to new karmic situations, and once they do, everything seems calmer again. So the family learns to work together and support each other through the times of trouble. If they get

धू

*To be spiritual is just to be, to allow other people freedom, to take freedom for yourself, to neither inflict nor allow infliction, and to remove yourself by your own authority from a situation that is incompatible by saying, "I'm not part of that."*

good at working with each other, they can actually work through karma more quickly because they will have more love to support them.

People sometimes wonder if their karma in a certain situation or with certain people is over. You will probably know if it is complete if there is a neutrality or "clearness" about the situation or person inside of you. To handle any karma, no matter the area or person, be loving and forgiving.

## Cycles of Karma

There will probably be times in your life when there will be more karmic situations to handle than other times; this is just how it works. Every life has cycles and changes that come with the cycles. When there are times of heavy changes, it seems that there are many situations to handle, and it can take much endurance to go through a karmic flow gracefully and with completeness. At other times, there appears to be more of a plateau, where things move along easily, without apparent turmoil. Both times may be right and proper and normal. It is important to learn to accept and work with whatever is going on, without placing out too much in the way of judgments or self-recriminations. When you accept, it is easy because accepting is not resisting; it is letting things pass through and saying, "Thank you, Lord, for another wonderful day." When you can do this, it becomes so much easier to break the karma free.

Handling karmic situations is like playing jacks. You have your hands full of jacks, and you can toss them out and decide which game you want to play. You can play any game you want, but you have to pick up the jacks. You can pick them up one at a time, and that is easy. Almost everybody can do "onesies," although it may take a long time to pick them up. But you never try for "allsies" until you have accomplished onesies, twosies, threesies, and so on. Then, when you have done all the easy ones, you have to go on to something more complicated, like "put them in the basket." You bring forward a little different skill, which tunes you up a little more, and when you have mastered that, you go on to something like "over the fence," and you learn to master that.

Children's games can be a lesson for us. Life is very much like a game. It *is* "for keeps," but keep it a game. If you land in the wrong square, you "go to jail," and you stay there until you can get a hundred dollars. Then you can get out, go back to "GO," and start all over again. But the trick is to know when you are through with the game; then you can put it away and go on to something else. In other words, the trick is not to get so caught up in the game that you think you *are* the game. You are not the game. You are much more than the game. You are much more than your present karmic situation. You are much more than the personality you express this lifetime. It is just something you play out until you are finished with it. Then you let it go, release it, quit playing, and the karma is released.

## A Karmic Flow

In the last section, I mentioned a karmic flow. Being in a karmic flow is not an easy situation to handle. It may not seem like it, but starting one is a matter of choice. Sometimes you hold on to something that is not for your highest good, even after getting feedback about that. The way it can often start is that you are already tied to the situation karmically, making it difficult to get out of—but not impossible.

People who are oriented towards listening to their feelings can sometimes have the most difficulty with this, as they are accustomed to listening to and following their feelings for a sense of what is right for them. The feelings can be a vehicle for intuition and spiritual guidance. However, when the emotions get attached and involved with someone or something,

घू

*You have the opportunity to change the karmic flow of your life through your ability to be loving. By loving the God in yourself and others, you can move into a path of greater unfoldment. Instead of looking at the factors of your life and saying, "That's my karma, so I can't help it," you might say, "That's my karma, and I will fulfill it so I am free." You don't have to blame your life's difficulties on karma. Through loving, you can complete your karma.*

they can create so much static that you may not be able to hear the quiet of your inner wisdom.

People who are oriented to the mind can also run into difficulties. They may have developed great mental clarity, which can become clouded when attachments or desires are involved.

The problem usually comes down to the level of attachment you have to a situation or person. Sometimes you just want someone or something so badly that you will use all your inner and outer resources to support you in getting it/them. If you put things into the Light and then hold on like crazy to what it is you want, then when the Light comes in, it throws up the negativity or attachment, and you with it. It is in your attachment that you open the karmic flow.

## Are You Creating or Fulfilling Karma?

Sometimes, a situation that is fulfilling and clearing karma may appear very similar to a situation that is creating more karma, but there is a difference. If you experience a situation that really shakes you up and you are upset and doubtful about what is actually happening, you may still be growing and moving right along your spiritual path. The best way to determine if this is so is to look for that little feeling

ध्रू

*You do not have to be concerned about yourself.
All things are already being taken care of. The
true self is moving you forward on your divine
destiny. You do not have to look at your past
actions.*

of joy somewhere inside, even through the upset, pain, and anguish. If there is still a part of you that says, "It's okay because I'm learning and growing," then you are probably clearing a karmic situation.

There may be other times when you are shaken and upset, and you will know you are not growing or learning. At these times, you are probably not releasing or clearing karma; you are just going through things that you have promoted, and to your original upset, you may add the judgment of being disturbed and upset with yourself for creating the situation. Then you will get to handle that later. Even if you are involved in a situation that is not a karmic release, do not judge yourself, do not put yourself down. Just go through it, get out the other side as rapidly as possible, and go on. Do not look back; it does not help. Do not burden yourself down with guilt and remorse that you are going to have to handle later. Just let it go.

When a situation is a karmic release, you will feel, within all your nervous irritation, a calmness; in all of your imbalance, you will feel a balance. This is not double-talk but is more of a description of what is happening on two levels of your consciousness. One level is ranting, raving, and screaming, and the other level is saying, "Go ahead, get it out of your

घू

*Karma is the inability to change an action or to act differently.*

system so you can move on. You let it build up; now clear the air. Put everything right while you have the chance. Finish it up so we can move ahead."

## The Importance of Clearing Things

There is karma on every realm below the Soul realm because those are the negative, psychic-material realms, and as long as you are living in any of the lower realms, you have some karma. If you had no more karma, you would leave the lower realms and be established on the Soul realm or higher, and only when you get in the Soul realm and above do you stand free in your own Light.

We also have karma related to our levels of consciousness. Emotional karma is emotional reaction, where you react emotionally to a person's body or expression, the weather, your boss, the traffic on the freeway, the state of the world—anything. To deal with emotional karma, you learn how not to react emotionally, and the first step is to observe.

Mental karma is going over and over and over the same thing in your mind. To break it, you stop that repetitive thinking, just stop it. Getting up and moving can help. So can doing spiritual exercises.

Etheric karma is unconscious, subconscious karma and is the most difficult to break because, by

ह्रू

*This life is very easy. Do and complete, do and complete, do and complete, do and complete—no karma. Say you're going to do and then not do—karma. Start to do and then not finish— more karma. Feel bad about all that—more karma. It's obvious we've got more karmas than we've got completions.*

definition, it is not conscious. We create etheric karma by repressing things, by obsessing, and by being "possessed" by such things as smoking, alcohol, and food. Doing free-form writing is especially helpful for clearing this kind of karma. (See Appendix 1 for an explanation of free-form writing.)

Even though you have karma, you can keep your own house in order, taking care of things immediately as they appear on the scene. When something happens that really disturbs you, get up instantly and release it. If it is with another person, go to that other person and clear it. If it is something within you, go to work with yourself to change it and bring it into balance so that you are happy and comfortable with yourself. If it is on the job, talk to your boss and get it cleared, or look for another job. If you learn from the disturbance, you will be free of it. If you do not learn, the experience will very probably come around again and again, to give you a chance to clear it and get free.

Clearings can be very important, especially if you have let irritations and misunderstandings build up within your consciousness. You must be free to reach into the spiritual realms and into God consciousness. You cannot be restricted by resentment over how your boss treated you a year and a half ago or last week. You cannot be restricted by the remark

धू

*You certainly can release yourself from past actions through laughter. Even in your daily life, if you can laugh instead of taking umbrage at some of the things that people say or do, you are already free at that moment, and the situation can't hang on you.*

your husband made about the dress you made. These things must be cleared and balanced. You can do it two ways. You can go to the person with whom you had the misunderstanding and talk to that person about it, tell the person how you felt, communicate honestly and openly, and clear the air that way. Or you can simply release it within your own consciousness—just let it go, place no more energy out that way, place no more concern with it, and move it out of your consciousness. Either way will work.

An attitude that will help is to realize that people are doing the very best they can all the time, considering what they are working with and where they are. If your boss yells at you, maybe you should not take it personally. Maybe he and his wife had a big fight the night before and she threw him out of the house. Maybe you remind him of someone that he has had a difficult time with in the past, and some part of his consciousness is expecting the same situation. Maybe you and he have a karmic relationship where the job of each of you is to learn communication and love in relation to the other. There are so many possibilities. There is also very little use in trying to figure out exactly which possibility applies, but you might assume that there is a reason for his behavior, that it is important to overcome the block

घ

*The spiritual energy will flow naturally to the areas within you that are most "asleep." It will move to the next layer or level that needs to be awakened and brought into a greater level of awareness. Be patient with yourself in that process. Allow Spirit to do Its work without hampering It by making judgments and beating yourself up.*

(whatever it is), that it is important not to create a bigger block by putting out resentment, resistance, and emotions, and that with honest communication you can recognize where he is coming from, gain an understanding of his motivations, and come into a position of empathy and love.

When you reach into a higher consciousness, you come to the realization that we are all one Spirit in many different manifestations. So if you strike against anyone, you strike against yourself, and that action returns to you. If you curse someone, that curse returns to you–maybe this lifetime, maybe a future lifetime, but it returns. What you put out is returned to you. You might want to look very carefully at the actions, the words, the thoughts, and the emotions that you put out, to make sure that they are the kind of things that you would want returned to you.

We are responsible for our actions *all* the time, and, at the same time, there is no need to get hung up in past deeds. Awakening to Spirit involves paying attention to what you are doing in the moment, not judging your actions, and doing the best you can at the time. If you have memory of negative past actions, you can forgive yourself for them and for any judgments against yourself, and then be careful not to move into those areas where you know you

ध्रू

*When you're working directly with the Traveler,*
*you have the opportunity to clear the karma not*
*only of this life but of previous times, to finish*
*up in this lifetime and walk free. It's a great*
*opportunity and a great blessing. As you walk*
*through the karma, however, it can appear to be*
*very strange. Your challenge is to maintain the*
*focus of Spirit, Light, and Sound, and just keep*
*moving steadily forward in that direction, no*
*matter what is happening around you.*

might get into trouble again. If you do not have memory of the past—and even if you do—just love yourself in the present and be willing to move through your life in the knowledge that those things that are right and proper will occur.

## Working Out Karma on Other Levels

You may work out karma on the astral realm if there is some reason that it cannot be worked out here on the physical. This might be done in the dream state, and you would bring back the memory of it as though it were a dream. Or it could take place in an awake state.

Let me give you an example. Once I was talking to a male medical doctor who related to me a very interesting experience. He told me that he had recently delivered twins. I said, "Well, so what? That's your job."

He said, "No, I don't mean that I delivered a woman of twins. I had twins." I asked him to explain more, since that sounded like a medical phenomenon, to say the least. He told me that a woman who had been a patient of his for some time had become pregnant. About the time she was three or four months pregnant, she and her family moved away, so he recommended another obstetrician who could take care of her and deliver the baby.

A number of months later (it turned out to be at the time she was giving birth to her twins), the doctor went into what he could only describe as severe labor pains. And not only did he feel as if he had delivered one child but he felt as if he had delivered two. His nurse was aware of all this because he was not sure whether to call an ambulance and go to the hospital or just stay at the office. He was pretty sure he was not having a heart attack because the pain was not in that area. He thought for a while that maybe he was having an intestinal attack of some kind, but he was aware that it probably was not that, either. But he was in tremendous pain for quite a while.

After the pain let up and he was talking to his nurse, he said, "You know, I hate to say this, but I feel like I just had twins."

She laughed and said, "You know, Doctor, it isn't unusual for a father to go through sympathy pains when his wife is having a baby."

He said, "But my wife's not having a baby. She's not even pregnant." The experience ended, and they both forgot about it until he heard from his former patient, who told him that she had delivered twins. He checked the time, and his experience was within the same period of time that she had delivered. He feels certain (and there is evidence to verify this) that he had "tuned in" and had an affinity with this woman and that he had experienced this birth the way that she experienced it.

In checking into his past-life experiences, I did see one lifetime where he, as a female, had produced a karmic situation in a very similar pattern but had not resolved it. In this present lifetime, he was involved in consciously breaking the incarnation pattern, so it was important for him to have this experience in order to finish up the karma and to tie up the loose ends so he could go freely. Being male this lifetime, he could not have the experience of childbirth directly, so he experienced giving birth as a psychic function.

The doctor said, "It was real; it was painful," yet the woman who was delivering the twins did not have pain because she was under an anesthetic. He had taken some aspirin and finally had given himself a shot of something to stop the pain, but it did not help. It did not stop the pain because it was not a physical pain; it was a psychic pain. That experience of pain was part of the karmic release and was necessary to the experience. It helped him to have the conscious knowledge of what the karmic situation was and why he had experienced it. But the conscious knowledge was not as necessary to

घ्

*Some people have asked me if there is a way to tune in to past lives and understand those experiences. Yes, there is, but why bother? This is the time God created and prepared for you, and if you live this life (in terms of living it, not just existing in it), the applicable past lives can become present in this one in such a way that negative blocks can be dispensed with automatically.*

releasing the karma as just having the experience and going through it.

## Why Do Bad Things Happen?

Unexplainable things often happen to people, and we wonder why: why them, how could people do something like that, why did God allow it? Here are some situations that can seem difficult and even horrendous when looked at one way, but when the karma of the situation is understood, a whole new dimension is added.

If a child is born deformed, blind, or deaf, it may cause great distress within the family and sometimes within society. The action of karmic fulfillment can explain many of these instances. Let's look at some possible examples. In ancient times, a person was sometimes punished by having a hand cut off or a tongue cut out. If the one who performed these punishments got caught up in the experience to the point that he did it unnecessarily, for pleasure, or unjustly, even according to the laws at that time, he might very well find himself in his next incarnation being born without a hand or arm or unable to speak. He would be allowed that experience to gain the understanding of what it was like and thereby fulfill the karmic debt.

If a person perpetrated a form of sadism in one life, that person might be the child or the spouse of a sadist the next lifetime or a later one. The possibilities are complex and infinite and depend on many, many variables of situation, attitude, intent, etc. But the law of karma says that there will be perfect justice.

Another example is the Vietnam War. Let's look at the Vietnamese people for the last three thousand periods of their existence. As a collective group, they may have got exactly what they created for themselves, and they may have balanced all of their karma. Is it bad for them to be karmically free of all that? Is that wrong? Perhaps that particular freedom did not come about in a way that we all might have wanted it to come, but it came about in a way that was entirely perfect when looked at from the perspective of the working out of karma. There was no overkill; there was no underkill.

The Americans who went to Vietnam and were caught up in it were part of that Vietnamese process many years ago, and even though they were born in the United States in this life, they were pulled back there to complete their karma. And those who went through the war unharmed were not part of the process and came home safely. So how can that action be judged as "wrong"? It is balanced, and now those people can progress even more rapidly because they have paid back the debt that they accrued at another time.

Am I saying to dismiss people's suffering by saying, "Well, it's their karma"? Not at all. People need your love and compassion, your reaching out and your caring. In fact, when you understand how the law of karma works, you may find yourself being even more accepting, forgiving, and loving.

An approach to war and other extremely disturbing situations might be to say, "Based on what I'm seeing right now, I don't like it that they are fighting and killing each other. I can't do much about it from where I am, and being righteously indignant won't help, so I think I'll just go within to that peaceful place and stay centered. Then, when everyone else is running around in chaos—emotionally and physically—I will be able to assist them because I'll be calm." In the midst of confusion and chaos, it is always helpful to suspend judgment and say, "I don't know what's going on, but when it's over, I'll do what I can to assist those people who have been involved in the turmoil." It is nice to just assist, not to try to punish or attempt to make anyone see any particular point of view. It helps to lift

घू

*Love your karma. It is your opportunity to learn. It is your opportunity to gain wisdom.*

people and give them the vision of unity, brother-hood, and oneness.

## How to Go Through Karma

Problems are beautiful because every time you handle or overcome a problem, your wisdom and your knowledge grow. Every time you overcome something, you grow. The problems give you strength to go further. Your karmic situations are your stepping-stones.

The earth is a classroom and everyone here is a student. The experiences that come your way, the problems that come your way, are your lessons. So every person you meet is your teacher. If you can keep that in mind as you are going through your day-to-day activities, you may be able to make some tremendous changes and grow very rapidly in your awareness. You keep learning and progressing through each experience so that you can graduate, because if you fail, you are going to have to repeat the grade. And if that is what it takes, that is also okay.

When you are dealing with any karmic pattern or situation, your time and focus are much better spent on loving *everything* in your current life and not trying to go back and figure out or change any-thing in the past that might be connected to the

धू

*By loving even your negative creations, you can*
*shift their energy and release karma.*

karmic situation. Spirit is present in each step you take and each movement you make. If you bring your awareness to that each second, you are doing far more for yourself than you would do if you tried to look into the past for causes, reasons, and so on. And, of course, if any memory comes up, you can do any forgiveness that is needed, bring loving to the memory and yourself, and then get on with your life and with loving everything in your life.

When you know of the law of karma (the law of cause and effect), you know that if someone does something to you that you think is unfair, you can just let it go. You know that if it *is* unfair, the other person will be held accountable for that, through Spirit. You do not have to do anything. You do not have to seek revenge or try to get even. You do not even have to think about it or hang on to the experience at all. You can just learn whatever you can from it, let it go, and go on to your next experience.

If you do not enter into the negative expressions of revenge, hurt, despair, etc., you will keep yourself open and present for your next experience, which may be a beautiful one. If you do go into the negative aspects, you may block the next experience that is coming forward. It is very important to keep moving in your consciousness and not hang

घृ

*"As you sow, so also shall you reap" is too often interpreted as a negative warning. It can also be a highly spiritual action, where a positive action leads to a positive result. Hold on to the image of what you want. On the physical, imaginative, and spiritual levels, create and express that which is positive and uplifting, and then you can reap what you have sown.*

on to old hurts and pains. Let them go as soon as possible, and get on with the business of living. You will find your life much more enjoyable and much happier.

## How Not to Create More Karma

The way not to create more karma is to do all things in God's name. Place the Light ahead of you in all that you do. Ask always that your actions be for the highest good. You may accrue some karma, but it will be worked off that night in the sleep state and cleared instantly through the actions of the Mystical Traveler.

This works only if your actions reflect living love, not ego involvement. The best way not to accrue karma is to remain neutral, where you really do feel and think, "I don't care; it doesn't matter." When you've reached that state (say with money, relationships, or anything else), you are what we call living free, and at that point you are probably getting very close to getting off the wheel of incarnation. But any place you have a hang-up, no matter where it is, you must work to become neutral.

If you make a mistake, don't feel guilty about it; if possible, go back and clear the mistake. If you have a misunderstanding with someone, just talk to them and clear it with them. As I have said, karma is usually produced more by guilt than by the actions themselves. So it would appear that the best approach is to either enjoy it or don't do it.

When you have done one negative thing—like yelling at someone angrily—it takes twenty-five positive things to neutralize it. Not to erase it, but to neutralize it. But instead of being under the law, you can come under grace. This would be something like, "I didn't know better, or I would have done better. They didn't know better, or they would have done better. And in that, I forgive myself and I forgive them. I love me, I love them, and now we move on." The Soul energy then comes forward and suspends it. It is not just neutralized. It is suspended through grace, and the loving attitude dissolves it.

So, you may not have to balance every little thing exactly. The idea of needing to exactly balance everything is the idea of "an eye for an eye and a tooth for a tooth" (Exodus: 21:24). The Christ action through Jesus changed that to grace. (There is more on this in chapter 10, Christ.) The key to grace is forgiveness—continual forgiveness—and it continues until your last breath. A lot of the things we have remembered keep us here, and we may not be able to get rid of them until we are through with our work here; that is, until we die physically. Being in a constant state of forgiveness is being in a state of grace.

We live in grace already because "the blessings already are," yet most people are not fully aware of it. To *know* you are living in grace is a by-product of Soul Transcendence and knowing—really *knowing*—that God dwells within you and within each person.

## Co-Creating with God

This chapter started out talking about human beings as creators, and I want to return to that idea. The things that you place in your mind as your wants and your desires, the things that you dream for and create in your imagination, become realities at some point, on some level. It is wise (to say the least) to be careful about the images you create and to which you give energy. But as long as you are going to place out a desire or a pattern of wishful thinking, you might as well place out the one that you really want. Is it God consciousness? The higher realms? Soul awareness?

What does a Soul look like? It could look like a purple ball or a white or gold one. It could look like the picture of a master, a picture of Jesus, Buddha, or Krishna. As you put that image in front of you, it can start erasing the energy from the lower wishful thinking that you have created (like the desire for

घृ

*If you are letting your fears and insecurities run you, turn around and confront them. Face them. Devour them. Consume them. Do it so well and so enthusiastically that you clear all your karma. That's liberation! And that's moving into God consciousness.*

the new car, the great sex life, the money, etc.). You can program out the lower desires and start placing higher ideals in front of you. Your mechanisms for success will start pulling you right into the ideal. You can assume you are going to reach it because if that is what you keep in front of you, you will.

The Bible says the idea that "as a man thinketh in his heart, he becomes" (Proverbs 23:7). That expresses a lot of truth when perceived from the mystical consciousness. And it works both ways—positive and negative. You may say, "The thing that I feared most has come upon me." But the thing that you fear most, you tend to think about. You tend to give energy into it. You tend to dwell on it and think, "What would happen if . . . ," and you can create that which you fear. It can appear because you have created it and brought it forward.

Then you may say, "Why me, Lord?" And if you can get the Lord to communicate, He may answer, "Why not? You created it. You're responsible for it." So you might just as well take a deep breath, chalk it up as an experience and a lesson, and go on. In reality, there is not much else you can do. Learn all you can from every experience and just go on.

Creation is complete within the lower (negative) realms. Co-creating in our everyday lives refers to

झू

*God dwells within you, as you; all you need do is awaken to His presence, and one way to do that is to listen within yourself to His loving direction. Ask for God's will to be manifested through you, and then listen for God's voice to speak in your heart.*

living this life with God as our partner. We are creating all the time, sometimes consciously and sometimes unconsciously, and when we consciously live with God as our partner and bring Spirit into our lives in greater and greater ways, we are co-creating with God on this level. And on the physical level, God needs us as much as we need God because God gets things done here through the physical body.

In the positive realms (Soul and above), creation is not complete, and we are learning to be responsible co-creators with God. In another form, you could work in another dimension, another universe. If you have elevated yourself in a certain way within a certain schooling pattern, you could reside within a higher realm. The final state of the Soul is to become a co-creator in the oneness of Spirit.

## Q&A About Karma

**Q: If someone is starving (to use an extreme situation), are we interfering with their karma if we send them food?**

A: We aren't interfering with their karma. As an analogy, say someone is drowning. If their karma is to leave the body then and if we try to save them, they'll still go. Don't worry about whether to save them. Do what you can.

**Q: If somebody asks me for advice and I say, "I don't know, but this is a way I might do it if I were in this situation," would I be picking up karma from them?**

A: It's possible that you could do this, but for the most part, if you give the person two or three suggestions, they can accept them or not, and you probably won't be as attached. All you say is, "This is how I see it. If you see it differently, God bless you, that's fine. This is the point of view I'm working from." If the person doesn't want to work from that point of view, they'll find another way. It's a big world.

**Q: I have gone through a number of challenging situations in my life. What was my karma?**

A: It doesn't really matter or make a whole lot of difference what the karma was. The important thing is that you go *through* those things and move into a greater spiritual focus and loving in your life. If it's ever beneficial for you to know the karma, you may get the information. Until then (which may never come to you in this life), it's best not even to ask a question like that, simply because it does not give you any information you can use to create more of what you want in your life. In addition, sometimes the consciousness can let go of the karma more easily if you are not consciously aware of the origin of the karma.

**Q: Are there any things I have done to my parents that caused them hurt and that I need to address in order to clear my karma with them?**

A: This applies to your parents and to anyone in your life. Ask them if you are part of any of their hurts and, if so, what part, how it came about, and what they want you to do (if anything) to assist them in healing their hurts. Then you can decide if you want to be part of it in any way.

**Q: Is there anything you can suggest for me to do to support my brother while he's in a karmic flow, or do I just leave him alone? I know I can't save him, so I'd like to be clear in my actions and not inflict on him or create karma for myself.**

A: His karmic flow is *his* karmic flow. You are not in it unless you insert yourself into it. Then it becomes yours, too. If you want more karma, feel free to jump in.

**Q: You told me that I still have karma with a certain person. Can that be completed from a distance?**

A: Sure. Most karma is just a state of mind/emotion, and sometimes it can be done in that level and not done physically at all. Yours can be done in the mind/emotion level, and there is no need to participate in the physical. And if you do decide to do anything physically, you can "call the shots" as to how much you wish to participate.

**Q: I am married to a man I love, and I am also in love with another man. It's very hard for me to sort out what to do, and things are so confusing. I feel almost crazy at times.**

A: You are in a karmic flow, and those are hard to handle. So is your husband and so is the other man you are in love with. If you put these three together, it is near impossible to handle. In this instance, there are three karmic flows moving at the same time, but not in the same direction. Conflict of an inner nature is the signal of this happening. Possessiveness and a form of material support are signs that it is also taking place. Part of this is materiality and how it is gained and maintained.

Don't be surprised to find out that a lot of the difficulty that will happen/has happened will come out of your husband's ego feeling rejected. You naturally have a larger ego. Most women do have a larger ego than men. Men need the ego support of women, and at the same time they can feel smothered by it and end up fighting the very thing that they feel they need in order to survive. When a lower ego decides to punish someone, you might not know it, as it may very well look like anything else or everything else other than punishment. Smaller egos pull the sympathy vote (as, for example, a recent president of this country did).

You are not in a rational situation. You are in a karmic flow. That is like lava moving downhill, and where does lava moving downhill go? Anywhere it wants to and even where it doesn't want to. But it does flow, and it doesn't even know it is doing it. So what does that say to your situation? Watch, listen, think, and then do. The karmic flow is just "do, do, do." There is no "do, be, do, be, do." It never gets to "be." It is over after "do."

Also, lava gets extremely hot and can burn everything in its path, and its path is a wasteland. One of the best things you can do is get rid of your pedestals that are inside of you and make sure you don't put anyone on them, as the lava flow will cut them off and they go anyway.

**Q: I went through a very hard time recently, where I almost wished I were dead. Was I clearing karma?**

A: You went through a real karmic darkness. You were working off extreme, severe things from

घू

*When you stop mentalizing and ask from your heart for Spirit's Light to be with you, things around you change. Then those things that seem so locked in and crystallized can be released and altered. It's a great day when you recognize that the things in your life that seem inalterable can be lifted.*

another time. If you were to know here in your mind what you did then, you might not want to live anymore. But without having the vision of what it was, you had to have enough of that come through so that you didn't want to live. The karma was severe, and it chose to come in on its own timing, so it was a hard task for you.

You tried to keep it quiet and hold it in instead of immediately going to someone and saying, "Look, I'm having these depressed feelings. I don't know where they're coming from. My God, I'm closed down." A counselor could have done therapy with you to help lift your consciousness and refocus it while this karmic thing was thrashing itself out in the darkness behind you. You'd have known it was going on because of the uncomfortableness, but you wouldn't have had the tribulations inside yourself.

**Q: I'm concerned that I am creating negative karma for myself and leaving the path of grace.**

A: Everything a person does makes both positive and negative karma, though rarely equally. Your attitude is more important than the action. And in whatever you do, be loving and choose wisely. Disturbing action creates karma. Disturbing reaction perpetuates karma. When you change disturbing

ॐ

If, indeed, you can be taught, the Soul will awaken itself on the physical level and dissolve all karmic bondage. Then you will be aware of the Soul on this level and on all other levels. At that moment, you become what we call one of the "living free."

action to loving action and disturbing reaction to acceptance and understanding, you may experience love, joy, peace, and fulfillment. These divine attributes help maintain the harmony of God's creation.

## For More Information

*For an explanation of personal-use and public-use MSIA materials, please see page 1.*

"Are You Relating to Karma or Spirit?" (SAT #7408). How karma works in you and how you can choose out of karma and into Spirit.

"Knowing Your God Essence" (Public audio seminar #7391). An excellent explanation of how to handle your karma.

"What's Commanding My Attention?" (SAT #4017). How to be objective about what you see, hear, and experience.

*Living in Grace* (Public CD set, ISBN: 978-1-893020-38-2). Among four CDs in this key packet are the seminar "Are You Living under Law or Grace?" and the "Meditation on Forgiveness."

ॠ

*You are becoming totally aware and completely capable of maintaining multidimensional awareness. You are already in Soul consciousness right now. You don't need to do anything except recognize it. You're there.*

"The Discipline of Liberation" (Personal-use audio seminar #3203). When you love, karma can be dissolved.

*Forgiveness: The Key to the Kingdom* (Paperbound book, ISBN: 978-0-914829-62-9). Forgiveness is truly the key to going through and clearing karma.

ध्रू

## CHAPTER 6

# THE LIGHT

*The Light is the energy of Spirit that pervades all levels of consciousness. It is an energy that is of God. It is pure, uncorrupted, and available for our use.*

## Introduction

Spirit is energy, the force that activates the human consciousness and gives it life. Spirit individualizes itself as Soul and so resides closely within each consciousness. Many people have said that a human being has a Soul, but it is closer to reality to say that the Soul has a human being.

As I have explained, the experience of God, with which we are all involved, is made up of positive energies and negative energies much like a battery is made up of positive and negative energies. It takes both to make it a working unit. Present as the negative pole

धू

*The Light is in everything; it's in every aspect of
your experience and your expression. You have
never been less than the Light. The Light is not
sitting around, chanting, and looking holy all
day. The Light is the total beingness of all consciousness, on all levels, at all times. The Light
is everywhere. When you accept that, you've
made your first step.*

of this total spiritual experience are what we call the lower realms: the physical, astral, causal, mental, and etheric realms. Present as the positive pole are the Soul and Spirit as the pure energy of God. These two poles working together are what we call the Light.

The energies of the negative pole of experience are more apparent when you are here in the physical realm. This level is their territory, and they can be quite powerful. But as you attune your consciousness more and more to the energies of the positive pole, to your spiritual self, you find that the spiritual Light can override any negativity. You learn to bring all the levels of your consciousness into the flow of the Light; then the positive energy extends itself through all the negative realms, and you find every level of your life becoming a manifestation of God's love and grace.

The energy of the Light is the spiritual force that is present within and that activates all things. It is everywhere to a greater or lesser degree. The Light is more active in a tree than it is in a rock, and it is more active in a deer than it is in a tree, but it is present in all of them, although they may not be consciously aware of it. The presence of the Light is most active within the human consciousness, and the human consciousness is unique in its ability to

घू

*It is so much easier to walk in the Light. That's who you are in the fullness and the glory of all your consciousness.*

be consciously aware of the Light and to work as a co-creator with the energy of Light.

## The Magnetic Light and the Spiritual Light

There are two aspects of the energy of the Light. One is magnetic in nature and is an energy of the lower realms (up through the etheric realm). You, consciously or unconsciously, are an individual director of it. When you work with this light for your highest good and for the highest good of everyone, you may also activate the spiritual Light, which comes from the positive realms of pure Spirit (the Soul realm and above). When you activate this higher Light (also called the Light of the Holy Spirit), you can experience at-one-ment with God, and the results in your life and in the lives of those around you can be quite wonderful. In the lower realms, you cannot get the Holy Spirit without the magnetic light because the Holy Spirit rides on the magnetic light, but you can get the magnetic light without the Holy Spirit. It takes a greater attunement to get the Holy Spirit.

This higher Light (the Holy Spirit) will never inflict itself on anyone or anything and comes only when invited. It can be active only when you are consciously pure in your intent and expression. You

ध्रु

*When we speak of the highest good, we speak of the highest God form. We are not talking of the god of the stomach chakra or the god of the lower astral or the god of any lower level. We're talking about the God of all things.*

are pure in your expression when you ask for the Light to be present for the highest good. You do not condition the Light by asking it to do what you *feel* would be right or what you *think* would be right. When you just ask for the presence of the Light and ask Spirit to bring forward whatever is for the highest good, that is when you are Light—Living In God's Holy Thoughts.

The magnetic light is neither good nor bad; it depends on how it is used. It can be used, along with the spiritual Light, for those things that are positive and that enhance the spiritual evolution of each consciousness. The magnetic light can also be used in negative ways. It is the energy field that people tap into when they use the force of their consciousness to control another person or to bring harm or hurt to another. Spiritual law says that all creations are returned to the creator, so it follows that any harm or hurt you perpetrate will be returned to you, as we looked at in the previous chapter, Karma: Creation and Fulfillment.

Just as everyone is an extension of God, through individualized Soul, so is everyone the Light. All people have this energy of Light present with them to various degrees, and all possess various abilities to express it and work with it. Some people are more attuned to the magnetic light, and some are more attuned to the spiritual Light. Wherever you find yourself is fine. All the levels are steps along the way of your spiritual evolution.

## You Do It Yourself

One religious concept that has been prevalent throughout history is that the priest, minister, or guru is somehow special and has a greater attunement to the spiritual Light. Thus, many people look to a "special one" as the savior or the intermediary with God. In the last few decades, a whole new consciousness has been moving across the planet, saying that each person is special and that as each develops their inner spiritual awareness, each has the ability to become attuned to the spiritual Light through their own consciousness. So each person starts their own salvation. Each person becomes the teacher, the student, the worker, and the harvester of their own beingness.

Too often, however, people want to yoke themselves to someone outside of themselves in the physical world and say, "Do it for me." This will probably not work and will usually delay your spiritual unfoldment. This does not mean you do it all by yourself. No way. We are all connected, we are all dependent upon one another to some extent, and no one is going to do everything by himself or herself. You may want a wayshower, a guide, someone to point the direction, but do not let anyone do it for you. I do not do it for you. I show you techniques, methods, and ways. I tell you what has worked for me and what I know has worked for other people. But it could all appear to be a lie until you do it and it works for you. This is why I always advise people to "check it out" and get their own experience.

The position of the human consciousness is unique. God has given the human consciousness the ability to be aware of itself and to know God consciously. God has allowed us the position of co-creators and thereby given us the opportunity to learn responsibility to the Light within us. God has given us these beautiful realms of physical, emotional, mental, and unconscious existence and has supplied the magnetic light of these levels to give us infinite opportunity to create. We can create many things, and God has instituted the law of karma so that we will always be made aware of our creations. It is feedback so we will know how we are doing.

द्यू

*All you have to do is keep freedom in your con-*
*sciousness and be open to let Light and love flow*
*through you to everything. You don't have to say,*
*"God bless that flower, that ant, those build-*
*ings, that tree." The blessings flow automatical-*
*ly as soon as Spirit uses you as a channel into*
*this world.*

## Sharing Your Light

As the human consciousness moves away from the negative creations of the magnetic light towards the positive creations of the spiritual Light, it comes closer and closer to God and the Soul, that individualized spark of God within. Some people let that Light shine through their expression more readily than others, and these are the ones who are happy, smiling, and nice to be around, the ones who can lift you just by being there.

When you come from that center of Light, you expand your ability to love and to share with people, to reach out and touch them. You expand your ability to say in many ways, "Thank you for being here." Maybe you think you could not say that to anyone, that it would sound namby-pamby, but why ignore others when they really need a pat on the back and a verification that they are doing okay? Sometimes it is in the smallest areas that people need your Light and love the most. Sometimes that pat on the back and a quick, "It's really nice to see you," can do so much to awaken the consciousness of Light in others. They can suddenly stand up and face the day. That service of love may be returned to you at a later time, and it is nice to reap those rewards.

Many years ago I knew the principal of a high school who did not let his Light shine through very much. He would walk through the halls really down in the mouth, and he seldom smiled. Every time he was around, he created a lot of tension, and the teachers and students would think, "I wonder what's wrong? I wonder if I've done something wrong?" After a couple of years, he was transferred to another school, and the new principal would smile, laugh, and share his beingness with the faculty and students. When he liked something, he would say so, and when he didn't, he would suggest changes. It was amazing how the morale of the entire school lifted because one man let the Light within him shine out and expressed the love he felt for the people around him.

## Working with the Light

Wherever you go, ask for God's Light to surround you, protect you, and fill you for the highest good. Place it ahead of you wherever you are going so that you will always be well-received. And each time you meet someone, ask that this Light be placed between the two of you, not as a barrier, but as that which can clarify. If you do that, everything that comes to you will come through the Light.

Learning to let the spiritual Light flow can be one of your most rewarding experiences. That Light within you will guide you as you learn to attune yourself to its direction. If you get in your car and ask for the Light to surround and protect you and then you speed, the Light is probably not going to do a whole lot for you. It may be that the "white light" you called in to help you asks the "red light" for a special assist. But if you get in the car and attune yourself to the Light within you, you are probably going to drive the speed limit, be careful, and watch. Then it is very easy for the Light to work with you.

When you work with the Light, you walk within the most absolute protection that exists. It is so perfect and so absolute that you may not even know you are being guided out of areas potentially disastrous for you. Perhaps you get tied up in traffic or delayed in some other way and later find out that, had you been on time, you might have been involved in a tremendous wreck. You have heard stories of people missing a plane for all sorts of strange reasons, and that plane crashes, killing all aboard. This may be the Light in action. When you get delayed or caught up in some unexpected happenstance, you may never be aware when it is the means to protect you from disaster. So do not be too

झू

*The Light works the way it works. It doesn't always work the way you think it should work or the way you would like it to work. It is the most powerful force on the planet and the most powerful force in your life.*

quick to judge your experience. What you see as an irritation may be your greatest protection, the greater manifestation of Spirit working in your life.

You might think that if you use the Light as protection, you should be able to walk down a dark alley in the middle of the night, safe from all harm. But if the Light is really working for you in the highest way, it might not have you walking down a dark alley in the middle of the night in the first place. Instead, you will be somewhere else, safe from harm. Using the Light does not mean that you can be irresponsible in your actions. If you are open to the Light, develop your awareness of it, and learn to flow with it, you can find your life unfolding in the most beautiful, dynamic, creative, and loving ways imaginable.

You know, hindsight is twenty-twenty vision. You say, "I shouldn't have done that. I should have done this other thing." In retrospect, you know what would have been the right action, the Light action. Foresight is wisdom, given to the few who will look forward. But "heresight" is available to all who will use it. If you are living here and watching, you will not need hindsight because there will be no regrets, and you will have no concern for the future because when you are living here, you are adaptive and can handle whatever comes to you.

You can always handle the present moment; there is never any difficulty in that. The difficulty comes when you allow your mind and your emotions to split off into yesterday or tomorrow and dissipate your energies. That is what happens: the energies split and you think, "I'm really falling apart. I have to get more rest. I'd better get to bed." So you go to bed, and the Soul can then leave the body and go into an energy field of pure Light and regain the quiet contentment of pure beingness. The mind and emotions quiet down. Then the Soul comes back and recharges the body with positive, spiritual Light, and you wake up in the morning feeling much better. You say, "I really feel together today," and you are. The energies are all together and present in the here and now.

The eternal quest within everyone, even if you name it different things, is always towards greater happiness, greater success, and greater ability to do and accomplish. Sometimes it is called comfort, security, or contentment. Sometimes it is called self-realization, at-one-ment, universal consciousness, or God-realization. Whatever you call it, it is that thing that will work for you and bring you the joy you know is your heritage. It is very true that joy, happiness, and success are your heritage, and there are keys present within your consciousness that will unlock these goals for you.

## Light Columns

We have a guideline in the Movement of Spiritual Inner Awareness, which is to always leave something better than you found it. One way I do this is to plant Light columns everywhere I go. For example, many years ago when I was in Mexico, I climbed to the top of the Pyramid of the Sun and placed a Light column there. I returned a few years later and could see the Light column from miles away. I could see it as a big, shimmering, white-purple haze in the air above the pyramid. It had held solidly, and that was so nice because a lot of people got into the spiritual Light frequency as they climbed to the top of the pyramid.

This is how you can place a Light column: for the highest good, envision or intend a funnel or pillar of Light from the highest place you can imagine going right through you and into the very core of the earth. That is all you need to do. The Light column you place may be effective for two days, thirty minutes, or fifteen years. Its duration does not matter, and you do not even need to concern yourself with that since Spirit is actually doing it. Perhaps a Light column will

घू

*Placing Light columns is a way to integrate into*
*your daily life and routine a specific awareness*
*of Spirit. When you do that, you are using your*
*spiritual energy in positive action that can bring*
*positive results to this level.*

hold for two hours, which may be the exact amount of time it was needed in that area.

If you are in one area day after day, continue to place Light columns there. People who have used this technique in their homes and offices have noticed positive results. It is a beautiful and effective way to clean up your immediate environment. You can also do this throughout the city you live in. For example, it used to be that you could go up and down New York City and only see shadows, but now you can see a lot of Light there. I flew over New York City once and thought there was smog over the city, but when I looked again, I realized, "Good gravy! That whole city has a haze of white Light all over it." I sat back in the seat, tears came to my eyes, and I thought, "Somebody in New York, at least one, knows how to do this." I found out later that the MSIA ministers in New York had been all up and down Manhattan Island, in the subways and everywhere, placing columns of Light.

A lady from New York said to me, "Have you noticed in the last few years that New York's vibration has lifted? It's lighter, it's nicer, it's better."

I definitely agreed and told her, "I don't feel the negativity in my stomach and across my back. I'm looking forward more to coming here." It is nicer to go to all the places I have traveled to before, not because they are familiar, although that helps, but because the places are lighter and more vibrant, and I do not have to work as hard to get the energy up and out.

Placing Light columns is a way to integrate into your daily life and routine a specific awareness of Spirit. When you do this, you are using your spiritual energy in positive action that can bring positive results to the physical level. It is wonderful when more and more people are willing to say, "I'm a Light bearer. I'll bear Light wherever I go." As a spiritual being, you have inside the ability to call forth and bring forth the Light of God into any environmental situation and to transmute the negativity into a positive gain. As just one example of this, to help stabilize the earth, you can ask that a column of Light be placed into the center of the earth and then radiate to the north and south poles. This can help areas that are prone to earthquakes.

Light columns can be as big as a drinking glass, as thin as a pencil, as large as a house, as huge as an entire city, or like the Washington Monument. Have you ever seen the sun shining through a window and seen dust particles floating in the air? A Light column will sometimes look very much like that.

When you see that kind of Light energy or force, you may think your vision is a little disturbed, but it may be that you are tuning in to higher frequencies and seeing a little more than the physical realm. That is good news. Of course, you might not visually perceive the Light columns, and you certainly do not have to. Not seeing them does not lessen in any way your ability to create them. You will probably never know directly the benefit that such work has, the ways it touches to people, or the positive changes it brings about. It is a silent work, a silent ministry, and a powerful one.

## Q&A About the Light

### Q: How do we call in the Light?

A: We use the expression "call in the Light," but the Light is always here, so we actually call ourselves forward into the Light.

There are many techniques for asking for the Light, and the main idea is along these lines: "If this is for my highest good and for theirs, then I would like the Light to be placed with me, with them, and with this situation." If your intention is clear that you are asking for the spiritual Light for the highest good, you can also just say, "Light." This is the first thought in some people's minds when they hear a

घू

*There are a lot of ways to hold the Light and send the Light and work with the Light. One way is that as soon as someone tells you about a situation, just pass it right into the consciousness of the Light. Before that person even finishes getting the words out, the Light has gone.*

siren or hear about a situation that is distressing or challenging in some way. Some people read the newspaper and listen to news on TV, and in their consciousness is "Light" for all they read, hear, or see.

**Q: How do I "hold the Light" for someone or a situation?**

A: Ask for the Light for the highest good in the situation. Then, as much as possible, be in the situation neutrally. This means to be nonjudgmental and to simply accept whatever is there, even though you may not agree with it or like it. And be loving no matter what is going on.

**Q: What if I can't be neutral in a situation, but I still would like the Light to be there for the highest good?**

A: Just ask for the Light to be there for the highest good. *You* aren't doing it; *God* is doing it. You are simply asking. You can also ask that the Masters of Light send the Light to the situation or person. Doing that can filter out your emotional attachment to the outcome.

**Q: Can you overuse the Light by putting it around every action and working with it?**

ॡ

As an ongoing practice, it's a good idea to
place a Light column twice a day at your home.
It can help clear any negativity—not only from
your home but from the person who places the
Light column.

A: No, there is no way to overuse it. But you can underuse it by forgetting to ask for it. I'd ask for it *all* the time.

**Q: I've been attending meetings for several days and am really exhausted when the day is over. Do you have any suggestions for handling this better?**

A: With me, always, the first priority is for a person to take care of himself or herself. Always. During the meetings and throughout the day, call in the Light to purify and cleanse and to bring the spiritual energy more present. Also remember that you are being used as a battery for those less able to contact more directly into the Light inside of themselves.

**Q: Would you share a little bit more about Light columns?**

A: Let's just say that we should all be Light columns first. Physically, mentally, emotionally, spiritually, we should be a Light column. Then, wherever we go, wherever we sit, wherever we talk, we should leave a column of our beingness of Light there. We should project it collectively into areas so that we're riveting everything together like a cobweb of Light forms, energies that are intricately intertwined and as graceful as the most delicate lace. And even though they may sometimes look like a great whirlwind, sort of rough and crude, when you get into it, you find that it's a filigree and that each little strand is very fine. But together, like strands of steel wound together into cable, they are very strong.

**Q: If I ask inwardly for you to send the Light to someone, is that less effective than if I talk or write to you or call the MSIA office and ask that you do this?**

A: It's just as effective to ask inwardly. You can also write to me and burn the letter. It doesn't have to be done physically because the work I do is done spiritually, and it's done instantly, as soon as you ask inwardly.

**Q: I have heard you and others say "Father-Mother God" when you ask for the Light. I don't have a clear concept of Father-Mother God.**

A: It is the positive and negative frequency, the earth frequency and the Spirit frequency combined. We're not just saying, "Let's go to heaven and forget this world," nor are we saying, "Let's just live in this world and forget heaven." We're saying, "Let's unite them so that while we're on Earth, we can be in heaven."

Father-Mother is a positive and negative polarity like on a battery; you need both poles to make

the battery go. But if we asked for the Light by saying, "Positive-Negative Polarity," most people
would balk at the words. So we use common vocabulary that most people can understand and say,
"Father-Mother God."

**Q: If all things are happening according to
the highest good and in perfect timing, why
send the Light?**

A: Because Spirit will not usually look at a plan to
see if an alternate can be instituted unless requested
from this level of Spirit. In the cosmic sense, taking
all eternity into consideration, all things are ultimately for the highest good because not one Soul
will be lost. But very few of us function at that cosmic, ultimate level. On this level where most of us
function, all things don't necessarily happen for the
highest good or in perfect timing. So it's always
appropriate to send the Light—for the highest good
(which is something God knows and we, on our personality levels, don't always know). Sending the
Light for the highest good increases the positive
energy in a situation and increases the likelihood that
the highest good possible will take place, rather than
a not-so-high good.

Also, the spiritual worlds are quite polluted with
all the extraneous thought-patterns that we are

घू

*Keep it simple. Prayer does not have to be complicated. Remember, you don't have to spell out all the details. All you need to do is place the situation in God's hands and let God handle the results.*

heir to. Our job is to transmute these things that come in. When we get a down feeling or a negative thought—no matter if it's ours or someone else's or if we don't know where it came from—we transmute it in Light and put it back out as Light. Some of the metaphysical churches know this and are doing it. They have 24-hour prayer groups going, blessing and putting out the positive energy.

We also have Prayer Lists at the MSIA office and in various MSIA centers around the world. People place names on the lists, and whenever anyone asks for the Light to go to "the MSIA Prayer List," it goes to everyone on all the Prayer Lists.

Every little prayer or Light group around, asking for the Light of God for the highest good of mankind and praying and asserting goodwill and brotherhood, helps clean out the negativity we feel.

**Q: My dog has been very sick, and I sometimes tread a fine line between having a desired outcome for her (according to me) and keeping in mind the highest good of all concerned.**

A: Having a desired outcome is not in conflict with her highest good, as the Lord listens to that prayer for the highest good of your dog. And this applies to people, situations—everything.

ह्यू

*Each action you take, each Light column you place, each moment that you stoop to raise another or to send our Father's Light to another being, that action resounds throughout the universe, and the love and the Light available to all is increased. You have chosen to do a mighty service. I am most grateful.*

Q: Sometimes when I think of you, I will send you the Light or think, "God bless you." Does this help you in any way?

A: Yes, it sure does. Thoughts are transmitted over long distances, and we are affected on many different levels by them. Sending the thought "I love you" or "God bless you" can work wonders, and I appreciate it when you send those words or the Light to me.

## For More Information

*For an explanation of personal-use and public-use MSIA materials, please see page 1.*

*Joyful Meditations* (Personal-use CD set, ISBN: 978-1-893020-37-5). Among the four CDs is "The Light Attunement."

"How Can You Tell the Level of Light in You?" (SAT #7296). How we block our Light and how not to do this.

*Psychic Protection* (Paperbound book, ISBN: 978-0-914829-69-0). Great techniques for using the Light for protection. A "must" book to have.

घू

*It assists your Soul's growth when you silently*
*send the Light to others.*

*Manual on Using the Light* (Paperbound book, ISBN: 978-0-914829-13-3). Basic and useful information on the Light, presented with cartoon illustrations.

"The Light, the Truth, and the Way" (Public audio seminar #7571). One of J-R's early seminars, with terrific information on the Light: how it works, how to work with it, and much more.

छू

## CHAPTER 7

# SOUL TRANSCENDENCE: THE WORK OF THE MYSTICAL TRAVELER

*All that you want to be, you already are. All you have to do is move your awareness there and recognize the reality of your own Soul. And the message of MSIA and the Traveler is that God is in heaven, that there are greater realms, that you do not have to die to experience them, and that you can know the divine reality while you live on this earth.*

*The Traveler does not come and say, "I'm going to redeem you from your sins and save you from your negativity." The Traveler comes and says, "I don't care if you're negative or not. Let's go, because all that other stuff is going to fall off as we get higher anyway." It is a returning action, where we return to the Father.*

झू

*It is important to understand that you probably won't get an advantage over anyone in this world by having an open heart. All that is going to happen is that you will live in a higher state of consciousness while you walk through the lower levels. That's it. And that's enough.*

## Introduction

The Soul is that essence of each person that is a pure extension of God. The mind, emotions, and body are elements that the Soul has taken to itself in order to experience those levels of existence. In the course of your journey on Earth, it is possible for you to learn not to be held in bondage or restricted by your body, emotions, or mind. And when these lower levels are transcended, that which is left is Soul. Eventually, as the journey back to God continues, Soul will also be transcended, and there will be only God.

Through Soul Transcendence, you can move in the Soul body above the cause-and-effect fields. From that level, you do not produce more karma in your life, so this lifetime may be your last one in this field of consciousness. The path of Soul Transcendence is for everyone, though not necessarily at this time, and each person will walk it at the time they choose. So, it is up to you to decide whether it is for you now.

You may think of Soul Transcendence as a great phenomenon that exists way out of reach. It is not out of reach. It is right here, right now. It has no dimension, no time, no level, so it cannot be separated in any way from you at any moment. It is always present. When you turn your attention to

ध्रू

*The Mystical Traveler's job is to assist you in*
*breaking free of all the blocks that stand between*
*you and your full and complete awareness of the*
*Soul level and the freedom of the Soul.*

the Soul, all other levels dissolve, and you are completely free of the bonds of the lower worlds.

## The Mystical Traveler Consciousness

The work of the Mystical Traveler through the Movement of Spiritual Inner Awareness is Soul Transcendence, and to do Soul Transcendence, a person needs the assistance of the Mystical Traveler Consciousness.

The Mystical Traveler is a spiritual consciousness that exists throughout all levels of God's creation. It resides within each person and is a guide into the higher levels of Spirit, the greater reality of God. The Traveler can assist you in clearing karma, and its work is done inwardly, on the spiritual levels.

In MSIA, we call this consciousness "the Mystical Traveler," but it doesn't have to be called that. It was given a term so that it could be referred to in speaking and writing. Also, *mystical* means "having a spiritual meaning or reality that is neither apparent to the senses nor obvious to the intelligence," and *traveler* refers to one who goes on a trip or journey. The Traveler exists on all levels of consciousness and can go (travel) with people into areas of consciousness that are not apparent to the senses or obvious to the intelligence (mind). Before

MSIA came into being, the Traveler was referred to in some places as a prophet, an avatar, a spiritual leader, and so on; there are many names. It comes from Spirit, from the spiritual levels referred to as the School of the Divine or the Holy of Holies.

The Traveler is freedom, expresses freedom, and gives freedom. Because it is *free,* it defies definition, but we can say that its nature is love, joy, and uplift-ment. It brings health, wealth, and happiness on the physical level, calm to the emotional level, peace to the mental level, ability to the unconscious level, and the fulfillment of all the dreams to the spiritual level.

## Working with the Traveler Consciousness

To get an idea of how the Traveler works with people, you could think of climbing a mountain, such as Mount Everest. If reaching the top of it were your goal, you would probably want to climb with the assistance, suggestions, encouragement, and guidance of someone who has already climbed it and knows the way. The Traveler Consciousness knows the way "up the mountain" to the Soul realm and above, and it can guide and assist you spiritually. Still, though, the climb is always yours. You are the one who does it, and when you have given over to the Traveler Consciousness to guide you to the heart of God, you have given over to your own spiritual heart, because the Traveler is within you, as it is within each person.

A very important thing to realize about the Traveler's work with you is that it is almost entirely inward and is not dependent on the Traveler's physical form. So, to know how the Traveler works with you, you need to go inside. Trying to understand this with your mind is limited, although ideas may point towards an inner experience of this. The emotions are also limited, although love is one of the signs of the Traveler and of Spirit.

One of the key things to do to become more aware of the Traveler's work with you is to open to the possibility that it is happening. You need to invite and allow the Traveler to work with you. If you do not think it can work, it has to stand back because it cannot inflict itself on anyone. You need to have the wit to open your consciousness to the Mystical Traveler and say, "Do what can be done." Then just be open and watch.

One of the best ways to invite the Traveler to work with you is to do spiritual exercises and build the bridge into Spirit, and then you can start to have the experience. You can read or hear a lot of information and be told that you are divine, but until you *experience*

घू

*When you decided that what you wanted more than anything else was to know God and your own divine nature, to know yourself as Soul, perfect and complete, you created your connection to the Mystical Traveler.*

this, it will remain only on the level of information. The Traveler can bring the experience as you are open to it and as you are ready for it. (See chapter 9, Spiritual Exercises and Soul Transcendence, for more information on how to do spiritual exercises, their value, etc.)

Sometimes the presence of the Traveler can be relatively obvious. You may see a purple light (the Traveler often comes in on purple so it can be seen), you may sense the Traveler's presence with you, you may ask for it during a time of stress and worry and suddenly be flooded with peace and calm. The Traveler's presence may also be very, very subtle, and you will only realize by looking back over the previous six months or a year that things have shifted for you inwardly and that you have a greater sense of balance, perhaps, or a more loving, accepting, or compassionate approach to yourself and others.

When the Traveler works with you, you may also find yourself having to deal with areas of your life and expression that have been problems or that could become problems if you continue to ignore them. Since the Traveler, in reality, is in you as you, this is like that greater part of you saying, "Pay attention. You need to look at this. I'll be with you as you go through this, but you have to look first and see

what actions you need to take to clean this up."
When these situations come up, they can feel very
uncomfortable, but if you go into them with a willingness to be honest with yourself and an attitude of
gratitude (for the opportunity of clearing karma),
you can go *through* them and out the other side into
greater freedom. And regardless of what you are
aware of, the Traveler works with the votaries (the
seekers after truth) "25 hours a day, eight days a
week." And if you do not want to work with the
Traveler, it becomes quiet because it does not inflict.

The Traveler Consciousness will not violate any
level within you. You must willingly and openly go
along with it. It promises nothing except to work
with you spiritually. If you decide you want to follow another teaching, you are free to do that, and
the Traveler just remains dormant in you. Or it
may say, "You're not ready for *this* school; you
would be further ahead to go off and practice in
this other school," and you will be directed to that.
I have told people who have come to me, "Look,
I'm not the one to work with you. You have to
work with someone else." They may say, "But I like
you," and I may say, "I like you, too, but that has
nothing to do with what we're doing here. You
need to have this other training."

The Traveler has free choice regarding whom he will and will not work with. If the Traveler chooses to work with you, you are an heir to all the keys that he has, and you are under the spiritual protection of the Traveler Consciousness. Many are called, but few are chosen because few really choose back. They may play games, but the Spirit does not play games. It is not something you can mess around with. It is like unscrewing an electric light bulb and shoving your finger into the socket to see if it will shock you or not. You know that this is messing around and playing games.

The Traveler is a maintaining consciousness. That is to say, wherever you are in whatever you are doing, it will assist you. If you want to stay in that spot for an eternity, it will assist you to do that, and if you want to move on to other levels, it will assist you to do that. It is very flexible. I tell students, "Be careful what you put between you and the Traveler because the Traveler will help you get that."

If you are on your own, you are a seeker, a neophyte, and you must work off all you can by yourself. But part of the divine plan is that not one Soul will be lost, so after a certain point you will run into those people who have the keys to release you from the pattern of incarnation. They have the connection where

घ्

*When you are working with the Traveler, all things unfold in their right and proper timing. You can assist by loving yourself every step of the way, by doing your spiritual exercises to gain a greater perspective on what you are experiencing, by loving the people around you and treating them with kindness, and by living with integrity and honesty.*

they can say, "Elevator, up," because they do not have the karma; they have gone through it.

The Traveler carries all twenty-seven keys for all the universes (I have discovered over 108 universes), and the physical form of the Traveler here on this planet carries the Traveler energy for the planet. It is just a commutator to step the energy down, like a transformer. All it does is step down the energy and extend the power to you. You accept the power and you extend power back, and that power strengthens until you are pulled into the Traveler Consciousness and you find yourself working off negative karma in the psychic realms rather than here physically.

If a person chooses to work consciously with the Mystical Traveler Consciousness and to learn the path of Soul Transcendence, much protection and grace are extended on the spiritual levels. This grace may also extend into the physical level, as many students have found, although the Traveler makes no promises on the physical level. People often find that their lives begin to work more smoothly and that they have greater inner resources for meeting the challenges of life that come to everyone on the planet.

219

ह्रू

*The Traveler is here to awaken the Soul, to give energy to each Soul so that each one will individually burst anew into the youthfulness of Spirit and be an active, dynamic tool for the upliftment of everyone it touches.*

## Anchoring the Traveler Energy

There has always been someone on the planet who holds, or "anchors," the energy of the Mystical Traveler here so that all can partake of it. It is almost a mechanical action, and because someone holds the energy, the energy is available to all. As an analogy, apples on a tree are available for all who come by, because the apple tree is there. To partake, of course, you have to be aware of where the tree is and, also, to want apples. If you do not want apples that day, you do not have to have them.

After a kidney operation in December 1963, while I was unconscious (actually, I was out of the body) for a number of days, I started anchoring the Traveler Consciousness on the planet. The spiritual forces had been asking me to do this since 1957, but I kept turning them down. Then in 1963, they made me "an offer I couldn't refuse." They just said, "If you don't do this work, you will die." So I agreed. I asked them what they wanted me to do, and they said it was to take people into the Soul realm. I did that, and then I kept doing it with more and more people throughout the years. (For more on this, see chapter 11, My Work and MSIA.)

Since I started this spiritual work, I have talked to many, many groups and individuals all over the world, and always my approach has been to tell them that there are other worlds besides just this physical world and that they can know them—in fact, that this is each person's divine heritage. Many people have listened and some have heard, and I have learned over the years that my job is not to try to convince anyone of what I say but just to keep on saying it as long as the Spirit wants me to. More than forty years later, I am still doing this.

In December 1988, John Morton started being more active as the Mystical Traveler. I still hold this consciousness, too, and am the Traveler for all the people I have initiated (I did not "get dumb" when John started being more active as the Traveler). Both John and I work spiritually with students in MSIA. (For more on this, see chapter 8, Initiation.)

John helps hold the Traveler energy for us all at this time, and after John, there will be others who will anchor this spiritual energy here so that it is available for Soul Transcendence. It is part of God's plan for bringing all Souls back home.

# J-R

by John Morton

All my life I wandered where you are
I awoke wondering who you are
In each moment you appeared as my self
I heard you to listen
I saw you to vision
I touched you to know
Who I am
Your life defines my reason for being
You move reality from there to here
You live from here to now
You smile and I am joy
God plays hide and seek with you and I
You looking and I finding I am God-in-hiding
You remove what does not belong
You answer my questions with your self
We laugh because we have no other choice
You are the lead in this play on truth
You wear everyone's attire
While singing freedom's song
You teach me to dance with love leading
When our day is done we belong to just one
For the one and for the all
I am yours

ध्रू

*The Traveler is a direct tie-in to spiritual uplift-*
*ment. When things happen that are clearing*
*karma, don't become concerned or discouraged.*
*Just clean up the mess.*

## The Traveler's Help in Clearing Karma

People who work in MSIA and who are working directly with the consciousness of the Mystical Traveler have the opportunity of breaking free of the cycle of incarnation this lifetime, to become established on the Soul realm, to walk in freedom while they are here, and upon their physical death, to lift in consciousness to the high realms of pure Spirit. This is the promise the Mystical Traveler extends. Part of the Traveler's job is to help the students fulfill their karma and teach them to walk free of accruing additional karma.

When someone first begins working within MSIA, they may often appear to have more problems than they did before because they may be working through their karma faster. Not only past karma but the karma they create day to day will often be returned to them very quickly—within hours or days, instead of years or lifetimes. For example, if a person "blows up" at himself or another person and is "fuming" inside, he may go out to take a drive and find that fifteen minutes later the radiator blows up and steam fumes out of the car. Instant karma. Cause and effect. He handles it, it is over, it is clear, and he can continue right on.

Similarly, relationships that have been slowly deteriorating for years may suddenly collapse, forcing a confrontation and forcing the people to communicate and clear the air. The relationship may reestablish itself and be better than ever, or it may be over. In either case, it becomes clearer so that both people have more freedom.

MSIA students are taught to work with the spiritual Light, which originates in the positive realms of pure Spirit. Its energy is positive, and its force can be used only in love and for the highest good of all. It cannot hurt, harm, or destroy. But it can stir up negativity that has remained dormant for a long time and bring it up into conscious awareness, therefore allowing it to be cleared. (See chapter 6, The Light, for more about this.)

When a person first becomes consciously aware of the Traveler and the Traveler's teachings, they are taken in consciousness that night while they sleep and shown the records of their past karma and the karma that they will be working through this lifetime. At this point, they decide either to work with the higher energies, to follow this path of spiritual unfoldment, and to work consciously to fulfill their karma, or to continue their life pattern with a lesser consciousness of the spiritual realities and without the direct guidance of the higher consciousness. Either way, they still have certain karma to work through in their current lifetime, and they can choose to do it with or without the assistance of the Traveler Consciousness. (When a person meets up with the Mystical Traveler Consciousness in some way on the physical level, they receive the astral initiation, and there is more about this in chapter 8, Initiation.)

The Traveler works through grace, and whatever the Traveler does with you is done in line with your own path, no matter what it is. The Traveler always works with you according to your karma, and when you come into the Traveler's presence, that karma is often sped up so that overnight you could have gone through a whole dispensation of karma. This is why in MSIA, things go so fast and why people go through things so quickly—because the Traveler stands in with your Soul and gets you in high gear for a while, and you take off.

The night travel is the sleep state when the physical consciousness is at rest and the higher consciousness is free to travel into the other realms. When the Mystical Traveler works with you in higher consciousness, it takes you, during the night travel, into the Soul realm and then back through

ॐ

*The immediate result of Soul Transcendence is to rise above situations and see them in perspective. At that point, you don't have to solve anything. Your attitude shifts as you attune yourself to the Spirit within, and the "problem" dissolves. It's called releasing karma. And it is also called living free.*

the lower realms to help you work off the karma you have accrued. The five lower realms (physical, astral, causal, mental, and etheric) are lands of illusion. It is like being in a fun house with distorted mirrors: you can really get twisted around and lost in the experience. But when the Mystical Traveler takes you into the higher realms, it is like suddenly being lifted straight up out of the fun house and being able to see clearly where all the different paths are, where the maze begins, where it ends, which paths are the dead ends, and so forth. Everything becomes very clear, and you can see which path you want to take. When you awaken in the morning and come back into physical consciousness, you may forget the specifics of where you were during the night travel and what you learned there, but the essence will remain with you so you know you are on the right path. (There is more on this in chapter 13, Dreams.)

In the Soul realm and above, you are in pure Spirit, and there is no karma to work out. This is why the Mystical Traveler teaches Soul Transcendence. We reach into Soul and then come back down through the lower levels while still in Soul consciousness. That way, when you work off karma, you work it off from a pure state. The Soul protects the consciousness, and it is like walking through the manure pile in

229

hip boots. The Soul is involved within each realm so that you do not accrue more karma, but you are still able to do the work.

As this implies, you have karma to work off on the physical realm and each of the other lower realms (astral, causal, mental, and etheric). You can work out your karma here on the physical realm by confronting your karmic situations. Ultimately, you must confront everything; you cannot turn away. When you have confronted the problem or experience and have exercised your wisdom of choice, you can move from it. But you must come to grips with it. This may or may not mean confronting others, but it always involves looking honestly and lovingly at the situation and all those involved in it. You may need to do something physically to resolve the situation, or you may resolve it simply by acknowledging it and loving it all.

When the Traveler works with you, you also have the opportunity of working off physical karma on the other realms during the night travel. For example, perhaps you were a reckless driver and were the cause of several accidents in the past, but you were never directly involved. The Lords of Karma may have a rather serious accident in your karmic plan, a lesson to teach you responsibility on the road. If the Traveler sees that it is not necessary for you to have the total experience physically, it may be able to alter the plan and allow you to experience the car wreck in another realm. So you might bring back the memory of the car wreck through a very vivid dream experience, the kind where you hear the brakes screaming, feel the car going out of control, hear the sound of metal scraping against metal, feel the impact as you crash, feel your body being thrown through the air, and wake up in a cold sweat, shaking all over from the experience. That has been your lesson, and it has been real enough to bring home the point that you must drive more carefully. You have fulfilled the karma, but through the action extended to you through the Mystical Traveler Consciousness, you do not have to experience it physically or handle all the physical consequences of a major car accident.

As another example, if you have experienced a difficult time with your parents, moved away from home, and left many problems unresolved between you, you may find that some morning you awaken with the memory of being with your parents in a dream and telling them of your love for them and sharing with them your present happiness. Your parents may call that day just to say they love you very much. These things happen when you are

घ

*The Traveler comes in on love. Move to love, and you'll find the Traveler entirely present in your heart. You'll feel the Traveler behind your eyes, sharing your world with you. You'll sense the Traveler walking beside you, touching your hand, as you walk down the street. As you move to that quiet place inside, you'll feel the Traveler's embrace and know that you and the Traveler are one.*

working consciously with the Traveler. It is no coincidence, though it may appear to be. During the night travel, you may be releasing hurts and resentments that you have carried for years.

This gives you an inkling of how the Traveler Consciousness can work with you if you invite it to. The Traveler works on every level of consciousness, on every realm of Light, and it works with you totally to release you from the negative realms.

It is so important that you understand this: the Traveler is not something separate from you. It is a consciousness that is present within each person on all the levels of consciousness, and each person's inner journey is an awakening to the Traveler on all the levels, up into the very heart of God, the center of living love.

## The Form of the Traveler in Spirit

If you prepare an inner mock-up of the Traveler and you mock up (or imagine) John Morton's physical form, John or I can easily come in spiritually because there is already a "fit." If you do not know how to do this mock-up, then we may come in as a ball of Light. (Most people will accept a ball of light—a purple one, a gold one, a white one, a silver luminescence.) Then, when you get more familiar with that Light, you may see it as you, and that is true. That is the bigger truth: Sai Baba, Zoroaster, Moses, Jesus, J-R, John Morton, and you—we are all the same in essence. So it would be just as appropriate for you to see *you* coming to you as it would be to see Jesus or somebody else coming to you.

But since you deal so much with this mundane world and sometimes do things that are "jerky," you may not be ready to accept the truth about yourself. You may say, "Well, Jesus wouldn't do any jerky things, J-R wouldn't do any jerky things, Moses wouldn't do any jerky things," and so you may think that only Jesus, Moses, or J-R can come in as that spiritual form. But in reality, that spiritual form is you, too.

Moses and Jesus shared their teachings by taking people out into the wilderness or up on a mountain in Galilee. I get on television and write books, or sometimes people write things about me. It does not matter if what they write is good or bad, just as long as it is put out. You see, every knock is a boost, and it is better for some to be infamous in this work than not known at all.

No matter what goes on in the physical world, the Traveler's work still goes on. Spiritually, I work through the next physical Traveler (John Morton) with the people that I initiate. The ones that Jesus initiated have to be worked with through me, although they do not have to come into my physical presence. When I die, then Jesus and I will both work through the next Traveler because all Travelers have to have a representative on all levels. That is a basic ground rule.

The Traveler action is a catalyst. It keeps things stirring and moving; all the dross surfaces, and then you are responsible for scraping it off through your life activity. You may say, "Hey, this doesn't work," and you may move it off or you may move out of it. One day, you may realize that you have become the alchemist of your own being and that the gold of your being is present. That is not gold like we think of gold metal here. It is much rarer. You can eat of it and drink of it, and it will sustain you through anything. It is the gold of that spiritual form that you are.

## Q&A About Soul Transcendence and the Mystical Traveler

**Q: What is the difference between the Traveler and the Light?**

A: The Traveler is a wayshower that works with people to take them into the Soul realm. The Light is the positive energy coming from Spirit. (There is also the magnetic light, which works out of the

धू

*The next big step is for your loving to come forward*
*so you recognize the Traveler as you.*

lower realms of Spirit, but I don't think that's what you were asking about.) The Traveler channels the Light and the Sound Current and then rides on the Sound—and teaches you to do the same. And remember that the Traveler is inside of you.

**Q: I am hesitant about working with the Traveler because I don't want to submit myself to anyone else.**

A: I think you are wise to be wary of submitting yourself to any person. I'm not interested in having anyone submit himself or herself to me. When a person participates in MSIA and works with the Mystical Traveler, that person is, if anything, "submitting" to himself/herself, to the Christ within, to the God within. And that is really a joyous surrender to love.

**Q: I am not sure I want to be involved with MSIA because I don't want to have a guru-student relationship. Must I have that with you in order to study with you?**

A: I am not a guru, so you can't have a guru-student relationship with me. I am a wayshower. I point the way towards the Soul realm. You travel that path yourself; I do not do it for you. The relationship is not of this physical level. I do not enter into your physical life or tell you what to do or what not to

ध्रु

The Mystical Traveler is a special aspect of
the Holy Spirit. You don't give yourself over to
the force that is the Mystical Traveler. You
are it. It is the guiding Light. It is your own
inner guidance.

do; that's for you to decide. I am there to point a way
if you need to have a spiritual reference point. I am
there to guide and assist you in developing a relationship with your inner self and with the Light and the
Sound Current. Then, if you choose, you can use
these to become more aware of God. And all this
applies to John Morton as the Traveler, also.

**Q: I have heard people call in the Light and
ask for the Traveler Consciousness through
John-Roger. Is that how we should do it?**

A: No. When you call in the Light, call it in
through the Traveler in your own consciousness.
Claim it for yourself. The Traveler Consciousness is
in each one of us, so don't give it away to my physical
form or anyone else's physical form. Awaken and
strengthen the Traveler in yourself.

**Q: I just don't understand what the Mystical
Traveler is. I don't understand why some people
seem to worship you, and I don't understand
how you can be aware of what is happening with
everyone that you call your students. Can you
help clarify these things for me?**

A: From the physical level, there is really no way
to understand the Mystical Traveler Consciousness
and how it works. That's like trying to perceive the

ध्रु

As long as you create separation, you will be in separation, regardless of how close you are physically to your spiritual teacher or to your loved one. You can be in the same room and be separate if that is your consciousness. Or you can be a million miles apart and be entirely present, in oneness, if that is your consciousness. You create your own reality.

infinite with the finite mind. That never works too well. Where you'll grow to know the Traveler is in your heart. When that love becomes more and more present for you, it will work for you, and then the understanding will come from an intuitive place, not from the mind.

The Traveler lives in you, as you, as that divine part of you. So when someone "worships" the Traveler, they are actually worshiping the God that is ever-present. The worship never belongs to anyone's physical form or personality, and if it is placed there, it is incorrectly placed. Only God should be worshiped.

The Traveler is awake in those who are its students, as they are awake in the Traveler. So it's easy to be aware of what is happening with them. It's just like another part of myself. If all is calm, I may not exercise that awareness, but if there is distress, I know that immediately. It's sort of like a spider that sits in the center of a web. If there is any part of the web that moves or is disturbed, attention is immediately focused on that area.

**Q: I have heard you as the Traveler say, "I am always with you." What does that mean?**

A: The profoundness of the Traveler being with you is primarily that you're never alone. The very moment of your deepest, darkest despair is when the Traveler is at its best. When everything is fine, you don't need the Traveler.

**Q: In seminars, I've heard you say that you present the consciousness of the group. What does this mean?**

A: Actually, I tune in to the levels of awareness of the group and individuals, and I present the teachings so that they might be most accessible. The teachings don't change, just vocabulary and idiomatic expressions. The essence of Spirit remains. The important thing is not what I say or how I say it. It's what you do inside yourself with the spiritual energy that is present.

**Q: How does this work when you are sharing at a seminar with one person?**

A: I'll give you an example of how this could work. Say I am sharing with "Susie." At first, I move myself into the consciousness of Susie, who she is, so I am then seeing the situation as she is seeing it. But if I talk to her from there, that could be confusing to her because she doesn't have anything to reflect to her. So then I would come in on the Soul consciousness and start talking to her. If she couldn't follow what I was saying, I'd come down lower and lower and would also come out more and more so that I would become like a mirror to her. (It's not clairvoyance, because I don't think I'm a clairvoyant; I just know what's going on.) If Susie is lifting, she will pick it up really fast, and the rest of the information will flood into her from what we call the Inner Master, which is the Mystical Traveler Consciousness individualized within each person. She'd then see how everything tied in. If she was not lifting, she would need to reflect on this within herself afterwards in order to get the information and the understanding. It could take an hour, a week, a year; it varies widely depending on the individual.

**Q: Was the Traveler energy anchored with everyone at birth?**

A: The Traveler Consciousness is in all things and all people. Some are more aware of it than others, and it's still there even in those who are not consciously aware of it. Those who will work consciously with the Traveler in a lifetime have made the decision to do that before embodiment. Then each person needs to choose and keep choosing to be awake to (aware of) that anchoring/presence of the Traveler energy in them.

And, strange as it may seem, sometimes it's for the highest good for someone to go through a lifetime not being consciously aware of the Traveler Consciousness in order to have certain experiences that are for their Soul's edification. It seems as though some are to awaken to it in this life, and others are waiting until later. All that is fine because not one Soul will be lost, and there is no urgency in Spirit.

This path of Soul Transcendence is not for everyone at this time. It is for those who had it "written on their foreheads" before the foundation of the planet that this would be their time. They can default on the time, but they cannot be denied the opportunity, by me or by anyone else, because the part that set up the time is us in oneness. That is why this is not a hierarchy of one person running anything. The Spirit is running it all.

**Q: Why would any Soul forget the Traveler after having become aware of it?**

A: This can be a mixture of a lot of things: karma, being distracted, being inexperienced, the Soul's thinking it can remain connected to the Mystical Traveler Consciousness and then getting gradually pulled away by the glamour and excitement of materiality, etc., etc., etc., etc. For the Soul, this is not anything bad. To the Soul, this is getting experience, and there is no judgment attached to doing this.

244

**Q: Does the Traveler work through all of us?**

A: The Traveler is *within* each person. How much or how little a person is aware of and consciously working with that consciousness varies tremendously. The Traveler does not work *through* everyone the same way. Many people do things that are diametrically opposed to the Traveler's teachings.

**Q: I went through a very hard time, and I kept asking that the Traveler take the karma from me. It took a long time to go through this— at least, that's what it seemed like to me. Why didn't it end sooner?**

A: The decision about how fast to relieve a person's karma or how fast to take away something that the person is learning from has to be based on *the person's* spiritual experience, not the Traveler's. If the person's suffering is taken away too soon, they may not learn. Sometimes they have to get down to being sick and tired of being sick and tired. And then the karma doesn't have to be taken away; they'll just hand it over to the Traveler.

**Q: Can more than one person hold the keys to the Traveler Consciousness at the same time?**

A: Yes.

हू

*Reach out and embrace the Traveler in your inner awareness. Know that form as the essence of yourself, your Inner Master, which is closer to you than your breath, more real than any other level. Know that in the Traveler's love, you will walk straight into the heart of God and awaken to the pure form of God's beingness within you.*

Q: If someone is a Traveler, is the person always a Traveler?

A: Yes, unless denounced by God as such.

Q: I think there should be a woman in your organization holding the Traveler's Consciousness.

A: Everyone in MSIA holds the Traveler's Consciousness. I would like to see four or five thousand Mystical Travelers on the face of the planet being able to talk to people physically. But in a way, that's not where it's at, because you think it's a physical body and that's the big illusion. It's not the physical body.

Q: Will you tell us who all the Travelers have been?

A: Many people who held the Traveler Consciousness throughout history are revered in various faiths. A number of Travelers have allowed themselves to be known publicly as such, and they are studied in the class called Travelers Through the Ages, offered by Peace Theological Seminary and College of Philosophy. Other than that, I usually don't comment on whether someone was or wasn't a Traveler. A more useful approach would be to focus on your connection to the Traveler in this lifetime and the opportunity for Soul Transcendence that this connection brings. The Traveler Consciousness is eternally present, and when you connect with that reality within you, you are connected to the spiritual energy that goes directly to God.

**Q: What God was the God of the other Travelers, such as the ones in the Old Testament?**
A: The Spirit God.

**Q: Because they were Travelers, did they all worship and speak about the same God?**
A: The Travelers worshiped the same God (the Spirit God), but they did not always speak about the same God. They spoke to the level of consciousness that the people in their evolution could understand. There are many "Gods," though there is only one Spirit God.

**Q: If it was the same God, why does it seem that the Travelers sometimes gave different messages from or about "God"?**
A: Travelers have exemplified different levels of consciousness for the conscious level of the people they have worked with.

**Q: Are there ever conflicts between Travelers?**
A: There is only one Traveler, and it has many names, so there is no conflict. The Traveler now is

all the Travelers in the past. Personalities may vary a great deal, and some are very close.

**Q: How does the passing of the keys to the Traveler Consciousness affect me as an initiate? Will I be working with you, or you and John Morton, or just John?**

A: If you are my initiate, you are still my initiate, so you'll be working with me. Of course, a Traveler is a Traveler, so I'd be happy to work with any of them. People may be more comfortable with one Traveler's personality, so that may be the Traveler they like to work with. But, really, you are working with the *Traveler,* not a personality. This personality you have known as "J-R" isn't doing it and never has done it. It has always been the *Traveler.*

The best way to say it is that the Traveler through me has its initiates, and the Traveler through John Morton has its initiates. John-Roger has no initiates. It's just the time period when the connections were made.

**Q: Why isn't John Morton doing some things the same way you have done them?**

A: The Traveler's work is Soul Transcendence, and that is done almost exclusively on the inner, spiritual levels. The outer things that the Traveler does have varied greatly from Traveler to Traveler

धू

*The Traveler is very good at the inner. Some-*
*times he's not so good at the outer. Out here, the*
*Traveler stumbles and stubs his toes just like*
*everyone else because that's what physical*
*bodies do.*

over the centuries. There have been Travelers who have been unknown to most of humanity in their personality forms, there are Travelers who have been very well-known, and there have been a lot in between. The important thing is that the *Traveler energy* is here on the planet for everyone to partake of and use to go higher in Spirit.

Just because I have done certain things, that does not mean that John, as the Traveler, needs to do them. I had to discover what it meant for me to be the Traveler, and it's also important that John continue to find his own way of being the Traveler, which may be very different from the way I have done it. It may also be the same in some respects. It's up to John to discover this for himself, just as it has been and will be up to each Traveler to find this out individually.

**Q: I sometimes have problems with your personality, and I don't want that to get in the way of the spiritual work you do with me. Do you have any advice?**

A: There's no need for you to like my personality. The best approach might be for you to just get along with it—be neutral about it—and work with the Mystical Traveler inside of you.

घू

*What the Traveler does, he does from loving.*
*Even when he brings correction and holds you to*
*your responsibility, he does it from loving. It may*
*not always sound that way at first, but it is the*
*motivation behind the action.*

The Traveler Consciousness uses my physical form and John Morton's physical form to do some of its work here, which is how it's set up in Spirit. But the vast majority of the work that the Traveler does is on the nonphysical realms, helping people work through karma and become more aware of their own divinity. John and I are here physically as reference points to, among other things, help people validate their inner experiences and share the teachings as they come through from the Spirit. So focus on the Traveler in Spirit because that's where the deepest and most real connection is made, and it's this inner spiritual connection that endures beyond this physical life.

**Q: How do you work with us here, on this level, as the Traveler? Is it to love us?**

A: Yes, and that takes many forms. When someone is teaching, he often finds himself in the position of admonishing. Sometimes it's done through joking and laughter. Sometimes it's done through turning away from a person. Sometimes it's done in a very sharp tone. Sometimes it's done by telling them to leave and seek elsewhere at this time because they need another discipline before they can handle the spiritual one. These are all techniques that the

ॐ

*The experience the Traveler brings to you has to do with Spirit, with God, with pure love that transcends all lower levels and lifts you into Soul—and then beyond. The experience the Traveler brings you is Soul Transcendence.*

Mystical Traveler uses, plus many others. But if you remember that that Consciousness loves you more than you can hope to love yourself and would never bring you anything except the ultimate of self-realization, then you would realize that, indeed, you are already walking with the Beloved.

**Q: Does the Traveler work with a person on the person's own inner levels or on the outer levels, the ones that exist independently of the person?**

A: When the Traveler, as a consciousness existing separately from a person, works with the person, this is usually on the outer levels, though the Traveler may occasionally work with the person on the inner levels, too.

The Traveler Consciousness exists on every level of a person's consciousness, so in that sense, the Traveler works with a person on the person's inner levels. (This is what is meant by the Traveler within or the Inner Master.) This work on the person's inner levels is a minor part of the work. The major part of the work is outside of the person, in the greater part of the spiritual worlds, including transcending all the lower levels and, also, the Soul realm and going directly into the heart of God.

**Q: Sometimes I find myself longing to be with you physically, and, realistically, that's not possible. But I still really want that.**

A: Sometimes when a person needs to spend more time going inside to nurture their relationship with the Traveler Consciousness within them, Spirit will bring forward a yearning to be with me (or John Morton) physically. It's one of Spirit's ways of helping the person remember to turn inward towards the Traveler. So, your wanting to be with me physically may be Spirit nudging you to spend more time finding within you what you seek. And when you do, it will fill you more than you ever thought possible, more than any physical being-together could. Relationships on the physical level end; that's their nature. The spiritual relationship with the Traveler is eternal, so focus on what is eternal, and you'll always find the Traveler right there.

**Q: During the hours before my mother passed away, she "saw" you, though you were not physically in the room. An actual fragrance filled the air. The following day, I had the honor of personally preparing her body for the viewing. Again, this same fragrance was present— every flower—most magnificent and beyond description.**

A: The presence of the fragrance is something I haven't talked much about publicly. You picked up the Traveler in another way that is also valid.

**Q: What will we do when you die physically?**
A: The teachings are inside. And as people work them and own them and validate them for themselves, they don't give a darn if I'm here physically or not because they know what works. That's why these teachings have been written down in the Soul Awareness Discourses and recorded on tapes, so that when I go physically, the community will hold the teachings intact, and they'll be a tremendous light to the world.

There always has to be a Traveler here physically, so there will be a Traveler here after I leave the physical body. He may be in Europe or South America or someplace else, but you'll still be in contact with him. And I will still work spiritually with those I've initiated even after I leave the physical body. That can't stop. The next Traveler will take over the initiates that I have under my energy field, and they will be in contact with me spiritually through him. And if he is not available physically, my initiates and I will still be in contact spiritually, the same way it is now.

**Q: What can I do for you?**

ॐ

*Each day, you need to choose the experience of your Soul. It is always your decision. What it comes down to, always and forever, is the commitment to yourself. And that starts when, ten billion times a day, ten billion percent, you commit to the upliftment and the unfoldment that is your spiritual nature.*

A: Let your devotion to your Soul and your love be your gift to the Traveler. There is nothing else that is necessary.

**Q: Is the Traveler referred to in the Bible?**

A: Not by that name. But there is a Bible passage (1 Corinthians 9:19-23) that could be called the creed of the Travelers: "Though I am free and belong to no man, I make myself a slave to everyone, to win as many as possible. To the Jews I became like a Jew, to win the Jews. To those under the law I became like one under the law (though I myself am not under the law), so as to win those under the law. To those not having the law I became like one not having the law (though I am not free from God's law but am under Christ's law), so as to win those not having the law. To the weak I became weak, to win the weak. I have become all things to all men so that by all possible means I might save some. I do all this for the sake of the gospel that I may share in its blessings."

**Q: Can Soul Transcendence be achieved instantaneously, or does it take a long time?**

A: There is a record kept on each person of their credits and debits. To use a money metaphor, you may have a $5 credit and a $10 debit, so you need five more credits to balance that. Thus, you put in

ह्रू

The Traveler said, "Do you love me?"

The answer was, "Oh, yes."

The Traveler said, "Then there need be no more worry or concern. Take that love and put it into what you are doing. By putting love into all things, you overcome all things. I am in all things. You just haven't seen that yet. So you must look through the eyes of love into all that you do."

$5 worth of labor so you'll have something to balance that. You can't go permanently into the Soul realm with a debit.

Some people will come to me and ask for a spiritual blessing of some sort, and I'll check their record to see what they have been doing. It may be that they have to go through a particular experience first and that the blessing cannot be released for them before they have that experience. But if they have a $20 debit and a $5 credit and if they go through this experience, they may come out with a $40 credit. So even though the experience may seem like a pretty difficult thing, it may really be a blessing in disguise.

You can't reach the spiritual realms unless you work for them. All I do is tell you what's there. But you can work out many things in realms other than the physical realm. A lot of your karmic situations are worked out on the spiritual levels with the Mystical Traveler if he is working with you. Your debits can be balanced out in a hurry. You may go to bed at night and say, "All right, I'll do the work that has to be done." So you may be "sweeping the floors" or "taking out the trash" all night long. Sometimes it can seem unpleasant, but if you can do it with loving determination, you may get some credits for yourself. And you know you can go through it because

ह्रू

I doubt very much if the teachings of the
Traveler are going to save the world. They're not
designed to do that. They're designed to free you
from the world.

you know that you will never be given anything you can't handle. If you can remember that, things can become pretty easy for you.

**Q: I would like to know more about my karmic pattern this lifetime.**

A: It is Soul Transcendence, to live and be in the presence of the living God and to know that. The way to do that is spiritual exercises. The Traveler helps you work off karma, but you have to remember that as an initiate, your connection through the Mystical Traveler is your connection to the Holy Spirit. I am a physical body; John Morton is a physical body. The connection is not through our bodies. It's just that we have awakened to the Traveler Consciousness. And all the time we're with someone, our Traveler inside is knocking at your Traveler inside, saying, "Awaken, awaken." This is almost all it does. Then, when you awaken, you feel the difference inside and become interested in going up to see God.

John Morton now shares the Traveler mantle (the keys) with me, and we see to it that as you travel, you are secured on the levels of the astral, causal, mental, and etheric. Unless you turn from the Traveler, you are assured to transcend at the time of death. If you do spiritual exercises, you have a better

ह्रू

*Soul Transcendence is your heritage. Awaken to
the Lord living in and through you. The
Traveler's love is with you, and his heart awaits
your greater awakening.*

chance to open your eyes to see what's going on, but you won't progress any faster or any slower because the Traveler does 100 percent all the time. Spiritual exercises are for you to open your spiritual eyes, to see what's going on, and then to use that information here as much as you can.

## For More Information

*For an explanation of personal-use and public-use MSIA materials, please see page 1.*

"Impressions of the Soul" (Personal-use audio seminar #2060). A beautiful seminar on how to find the Soul.

*Divine Essence (Baraka)* (Paperbound book, ISBN: 978-1-893020-04-7). A profound explanation of the spiritual forces that work with the Traveler in MSIA, awakening to your God essence, and the spiritual work of the Traveler.

*The Path to Mastership* (Paperbound book, ISBN: 978-0-914829-16-4). The path of initiation, the work of the Traveler, and the inner path of mastership.

*The Wayshower* (Public audio packet #3901). Delightful stories about J-R's own "Search for a Master" in one seminar and profound information about "The True Self" in the second seminar.

ह्यू

*The Traveler shows you the direction and walks with you into your awakening. Everything supports your doing this—every experience, every person you meet, every place you go. There is no situation that cannot lift you and point the way into your experience of the presence of God.*

"When the Mystical Traveler Works with You" (Personal-use audio seminar #2053). The Traveler can bring the experience of God, which leads to freedom.

"My Kingdom for a Horse" (Personal-use audio seminar #4018). A classic seminar that includes J-R's story of when his guru sent him to buy horses, including his struggle to lift himself from the confines of his ego.

ह्रू

## CHAPTER 8

# INITIATION

*To be an initiate of the Traveler is to devote yourself to the God within you, to Spirit, and to returning to your home, the Soul realm, from which you originally came before you incarnated onto this earth.*

### Overview of Initiation

Since Soul Transcendence is the focus of the Mystical Traveler's work, it follows that initiation is central to MSIA. Students in MSIA are initiated through the Mystical Traveler Consciousness into the Sound Current, the audible stream of energy that comes from the heart of God. The Sound Current is the basis of all life and is often called "the Word" in the Bible.

I am going to explain initiation in MSIA through the Traveler Consciousness so that you can have some idea of how this works. And also look to your own inner experiences for verification and expansion of what I say here.

## Levels of Initiation

There are thirty-three Sound Current initiations. The first is the physical, which takes place when a person is born here on the planet. The second is the astral initiation and deals with the imagination; it happens in the night travel (the dream state) after a person has in some way come in contact with the Mystical Traveler. The astral initiation is not anchored physically at that time, and the person may do no more with it in their lifetime. The next initiation is the causal, dealing with the emotions, and it can take place after two years of study with the Traveler in MSIA. Then can come these successive initiations: mental (dealing with the mind), etheric (dealing with the unconscious), and Soul (which is who you truly are). There are also twenty-seven levels of initiation above the Soul realm. As you have probably noticed, these initiations correspond to the major realms discussed earlier in chapter 2, The Realms of Spirit. When a person receives initiation, they are initiated through the Soul, so in that sense everyone who has been initiated in MSIA is a "Soul initiate," though they are not necessarily a "Soul-level initiate."

## *Receiving the Initiation Physically*

At the time the causal, mental, etheric, and Soul initiations are anchored physically, the person meets with an initiator cleared by the Traveler to do this; the Traveler works spiritually through the initiator, but it is the Traveler who takes spiritual responsibility for the initiation. The person is given the name of God on that realm to chant inwardly (at the causal initiation, the person is given both the astral and causal names). These initiation names—or tones—are charged with spiritual energy by the Traveler Consciousness for each person individually. Each level of initiation has to be maintained—both after it is clear in Spirit to receive it and after it has been connected physically. That is part of what "eternal vigilance" is all about.

## *Sound Current Initiations and Light Initiations*

An initiation to one of the major realms, described above, is called a *Sound Current initiation*. A Sound initiation has to be given by a Sound master, somebody who has a key to it, such as the Mystical Traveler. In contrast, a *Light initiation* takes place when you move from one level to another within a major realm. For example, let's say you are an initiate on the mental realm. On that realm, there are the

ह

*A lot of people are studying in the Movement and want to be initiated. To me, that's really the thing. If you're not going to be initiated, why waste your time? Go do something else.*

astral, causal, mental, etheric, and Soul levels. There
are also levels within those levels, and levels within
*those* levels. When you pass from one level to another within a major realm, you receive a Light initiation. As you can see, there can be many, many Light
initiations within one realm, including each of the
twenty-seven realms above Soul.

## Studying Towards Initiation

As I said, before being initiated by the Traveler
into the causal realm, a person needs to have studied the Soul Awareness Discourses for at least two
years. (A list of Discourse titles is in Appendix 3, and
they are described in more detail in chapter 12,
Studying in MSIA.) The person also needs to be free
of any recreational-drug use for at least six months
before applying for the causal initiation, as the use
of recreational drugs is incompatible with a person's
spiritual study with the Traveler. (For more on this,
see chapter 22, Health.) People are asked to write
and mail a letter to the Traveler as soon as they have
made the decision to study towards initiation; doing
this is a way of bringing their inner commitment
into the physical world and lining up all their levels
of consciousness in support of their decision. In
other words, it helps them make sure they really

ध्

*You don't get things in Spirit because you think you ought to have them; you get them because you work for them. The grace of the Traveler is extended to you and will assist you, and you must still do the work yourself.*

want to do it. The Traveler then works spiritually with the person to clear enough karma that the person can eventually be initiated.

Some people have told me that they think two years is too long to wait for initiation, but these first two years of study in MSIA are very important. They give the person a chance to check out the Traveler and the teachings and to make sure that this is a spiritual path they want to follow.

Discourses and spiritual exercises (s.e.'s) are two of the main ways the Traveler works with people in MSIA. (See the following chapter, Spiritual Exercises and Soul Transcendence, for more on this.) It is a good idea to take time each day for spiritual attunement through s.e.'s and to do them often during the first two years of study in MSIA. Building a strong habit of doing spiritual exercises and spending time with the Spirit within can do much to help a person build a firm foundation and prepare a place for the tone that is given at the time of initiation.

The Traveler will work spiritually with a person as much as they request and allow it, even if that person has not yet received causal initiation. Specifically, if your intention is to work closely with the Traveler and to be initiated and if you ask for the Traveler's guidance and protection and then open

घू

*The Traveler's contract with you is to establish you in the consciousness of Soul. You can trust that like you trust the sun coming up. It will hold until it is completed.*

to receive it, it is extended to you. Your intention is a crucial element. Generally, those who are studying for initiation and have that as their intention do get initiated. There have also been times when a person asked for initiation consciously, but being initi-. ated was not in alignment with them spiritually, so they did not receive initiation. In addition, even if you write that you are studying towards initiation, you are totally free not to apply for it later.

*Mutual Commitment of Traveler and Student*

There are different levels of mutual commitment between the student and the Mystical Traveler. For example, studying the Discourses for information is one level. Studying the Discourses towards initiation is a greater level of mutual commitment, and the Traveler can generally work more closely with this person to clear karma. Then, when a person receives the causal initiation, a promise is made by the Traveler under whose energy field the person is initiated: the Traveler agrees to work with the initiate until the initiate has received the Soul-level initiation, unless the initiate turns from the Traveler. At the time of Soul-level initiation, that promise of the Traveler to the initiate is complete.

If an initiate dies physically before receiving the Soul-level initiation, the Traveler continues to work with the person (actually, the Soul) on the nonphysical levels, because the promise the Traveler has made to the initiate is that he will stay with them until they reach the Soul level, no matter if he or they die from the physical level, unless they turn from the Traveler.

*Karma and Initiation*

When you receive an initiation on one level, this does not mean that you have cleared all the karma on the levels below that. In fact, there are massive karmas on the nonphysical levels, and the Traveler works with you to clear enough karma that you can receive initiation. It is a little like boring a small hole up through a huge plank, through which you can move to the next higher level.

*After Soul-Level Initiation*

When a person receives Soul-level initiation, it is then time for them to clear the karmas on the lower levels that are still there, and the Traveler who gave the person their first initiation generally works with them to do that, although there are occasional exceptions. Almost all Soul-level initiates go back down to the lower levels and clear karmas there.

Sometimes, a Soul-level initiate and the Traveler will make the spiritual decision to work together in the realms above Soul. This is not a promise but is a two-way agreement, and either side (the initiate or the Traveler) can call it off at any time by giving notice to the other. This decision originates on the higher spiritual levels and has very little to do with anything on this physical level. In other words, an initiate may consciously think that they want to work in the realms above Soul, but this may not be in line with their highest spiritual progression.

Some people have told me that they experienced more challenges after Soul initiation than before and have wondered if this was connected to getting the initiation. No, it is not. Initiations are for the higher spiritual levels. For example, as a Soul-level initiate, you could reexperience some of the causal-realm karma that you did not clear when you were on that level, and you now have an opportunity to clear it. But, still, this is not *caused* by your having received Soul-level initiation—or any initiation, for that matter. You have karma to deal with in a lifetime, and it comes up whether or not you are studying in MSIA or are an initiate. In fact, it is *because* you are an initiate that you get to clear it and not carry it over to another existence, and working

धू

*Initiates know that whatever comes their way is for their continual awakening.*

spiritually with the Traveler can make going through it easier.

## The Traveler's Work with Initiates

The Traveler's protection is extended on the spiritual levels, and I do what is spiritually permitted for the initiates on the physical level. That does not necessarily mean that things will go as the initiate wants or that the initiate will not have to go through very challenging things. But my promise as the Traveler is to always be with the initiate spiritually, so when I say, "I am with you through it all," you can bet that is what I am doing.

The Traveler Consciousness is continuously working with all the initiates to assist them spiritually in their Soul Transcendence. There is no obligation on the Traveler to do anything at all on the physical level for any initiate or, actually, any person at all. The Traveler can sometimes assist a person on the physical level, but he always does it within what Spirit allows. If Spirit does not allow it, he would not step in and do it—both for himself (he does what is aligned with the Spirit) and for the other person (he does not want to take something from them that they would only have to go through another time).

When you get into the Soul realm, the Sound is the Light made audible. You can have knowledge of

the Light and back off from it, but once you have
tasted or drunk of the waters of the audible life
stream, the Sound Current, you can never live
without that again. You have set your foot upon the
path of returning into the Supreme God.

## Q&A About Initiation in General

**Q: I just got the Soul Awareness Discourses
and don't know if I want to study towards initiation. Have you and I chosen to work together
spiritually? Am I one of the Traveler's?**

A: The Traveler keeps extending and extending
to *all* people, and that is one part of the choosing.
The other part is that the person chooses back. If
you want to take the next step towards becoming
"one of the Traveler's," you could look into studying towards initiation. If you write that you are
going to study towards initiation, this does not
mean that you *must* apply for initiation. You would
decide that after at least two years of study in MSIA.
Doing this does not obligate you to apply for initiation; it means that you are checking out the teachings at a deeper level of involvement. If you write
this letter and then decide not to go for initiation,
there is no harm done to you in any way.

Q: I have been feeling more sensitive since my initiation. Do you think the two are related?

A: The initiation and meditating can make you more sensitive to what has always been going on around you, and you may now know it.

Q: I am an etheric initiate, and I have noticed that I have begun to lose or forget things and kind of "space out."

A: There is no tie-in between being an etheric initiate and these other things. If anything, the initiation revealed to you what you were doing, but it didn't *cause* you to do it.

Q: I sometimes feel bad that I can't go to certain MSIA retreats and other events, and I am afraid that it will affect my spiritual growth and future initiations.

A: Attending MSIA events has nothing to do with your spiritual growth. That's between you and the Traveler and has to do with clearing karma on the spiritual realms.

As an initiate, you can participate in retreats and other MSIA events inwardly even if you aren't there physically. All the initiates participate in these events, even if their bodies are not there. Those who are there physically help hold the energy so that the

धू

Remind yourself that you can move into the higher Light, the Soul, now. You do not have to wait for some future time when all your problems are solved and things are perfectly smooth. The experience of the Soul is here for you right now. You do not have to wait.

spiritual work can be done for the people there and for those not there. And, as always, it's through doing s.e.'s and tuning in to the other levels that you are more likely to become aware of your participation on the nonphysical levels.

**Q: I have had a really hard time lately and haven't done spiritual exercises or read my Discourses much. Have I blown my chances with the Traveler?**

A: As long as a person is alive, they have not blown their chances with the Mystical Traveler. And ultimately, a Soul simply cannot blow its chances—because not one Soul will be lost. It's like asking if you've blown your chances with God. The answer is no, because there is always grace and forgiveness. And to receive of these, you need to be open to them and willing to let go of any hardness of heart, pain, etc., that might be in the way of letting them in.

**Q: The greatest blessing in my life is to know you and to be an initiate. I pray there is nothing I could ever do to lose you.**

A: I can never turn, and the Traveler is in everyone and cannot leave, but it can be inactive. There is nothing you can do to lose the Traveler unless you turn from the Traveler.

ॡ

*If you don't "see" any progress, don't worry. You can't necessarily equate spiritual progress with the experiences in this world. Don't look outward at what appears to be the progress or experiences of others. No two people are alike.*

## Q&A About Getting
## the Next Initiation

**Q: I got a letter saying that it's clear for me to receive my next initiation. What makes receiving it on the physical level important?**

A: It means that the consciousness can hold the energy here in the body, and it also solidifies the initiation in the consciousness. An initiation to the causal, mental, etheric, or Soul realm doesn't happen fully until it is anchored physically.

**Q: I've been going through a challenging time recently with my work and my relationship—both at the same time. Is this clearing blocks so I can get my next initiation?**

A: Initiations pertain to the higher spiritual levels and have nothing at all to do with you here physically. They have to do with the Traveler Consciousness, which can work with you in the Spirit to move through the necessary lessons on those other levels. So, it might be more helpful for you not to set it up so that you think you have to accomplish or clear something in particular on the physical level in order to receive an initiation. A better approach is to keep an open mind so that receiving your initiation is not locked into your

ह्यू

When you chant your tones, you are singing the
song of loving that has been sung by the saints
and sages of all time. It's a joyful process.

idea of what you need to complete physically before receiving it.

**Q: Will initiation to the next level bring more stress and intensity into my life—that is, more than I can handle? Or could it do the opposite and bring me more reserves to help me handle what I'm working on in my life now?**

A: Initiation does not directly affect this life. Initiations are for the higher spiritual levels. As I've explained, a person has karma to handle in this lifetime, Traveler or no Traveler, initiation or no initiation. Also, God never gives you more than you can handle.

**Q: If spiritual progress doesn't have anything to do with what I do here on the physical level, why are we asked to do spiritual exercises?**

A: Spiritual exercises are a method and a means by which you open your spiritual eyes to see what you are doing. When you see more of what you are doing, you may be better able to cooperate with it. Doing spiritual exercises is a little like tuning in and receiving pictures of what is happening in the other levels. S.e.'s give you that glimpse that lets you know that everything is being taken care of so that you can pay attention to the level that you are on. (For more on this, see the next chapter, Spiritual Exercises and Soul Transcendence.)

हू

*Be very selfish about getting to your next level of spiritual unfoldment. Love everybody, no matter what. Love yourself, no matter what. Present yourself daily to the Spirit. Make yourself available. Come into Spirit's presence.*

Q: How will I know when I am ready for my next initiation?

A: You might have a dream or an experience in s.e.'s that indicates to you that you are ready for the next initiation, and you could write and ask about that. And if you don't get it internally, the Traveler will tell you externally.

Q: I wrote and asked for my next initiation, and you said it's not yet time for it. Can you tell me why?

A: When a person is not yet ready for their next initiation, it's almost always because there is just too much karma in the invisible/Spirit realms that still needs to be worked out, and that has nothing to do with this level. Also, a person can get the next initiation on the other side (for example, in the dream state) and still not be ready in their consciousness, karma-wise, to receive it physically. So they get a letter saying they are not yet ready for the next initiation. It's rare that a person receives the next initiation sooner than one year after the previous initiation, and it's usually at least two years. It can be longer, of course.

Q: Why is it taking me longer than two years to get my next initiation?

291

ह्यू

*Your connection to Spirit through your initiation into the Sound Current of God is more valuable than anything else in existence.*

A: There is no set time before getting another initiation, and it's all according to what is best for your Soul's progression. Also, a person has to be handling their personal karma in the physical level in a very satisfactory way, and then we look for initiation openings.

Q: I have been a Soul-level initiate for ten years, and you and I have agreed to work together above the Soul level, but I haven't received any further initiations. Is there anything I am doing to delay or interfere with my spiritual growth?

A: No. You are clearing karma. Be joyful.

Q: It would be inconvenient for me to come to the initiation appointment that the MSIA office wants to schedule for me. I mean, I can do it, but I have to juggle my schedule to do it.

A: That's fine. You don't need to come to the initiation appointment. The MSIA office will let you know when other appointments are scheduled—maybe in a couple of months—and you can see if you can come then, if it's still clear for you to receive the initiation.

Getting the initiation is each person's responsibility. It sometimes amazes me how many things a person will put in front of coming in and getting their initiation. On the other hand, some people have flown across-country to get the initiation. One man took a seven-hour bus trip to Los Angeles, got his initiation, and took a seven-hour bus trip back home that same day. Another person traveled for four days—by foot, donkey cart, and bus—to get to his initiation appointment in another country. So I don't have a lot of sympathy when people complain about a two-hour drive or say the appointment is too early in the morning or inconvenient. It doesn't matter to me if you get your initiation, but I would think it would matter a whole lot to you.

**Q: I would like you, personally, to do my initiation.**

A: The Traveler Consciousness does all the initiations. The initiator stands and does the best they can, but they do not "do" the initiation. Get it very clear. The Mystical Traveler Consciousness does the initiations.

## Q&A About the Initiation
### Going Inactive

**Q: I was subscribing to Discourses for about seven years and got my first and second initiations. Then I stopped reading the Discourses for a couple of years. When I wanted to read**

**Discourses again, I got a letter from the MSIA office telling me that I needed to start over on Discourse 1 and that my initiation was inactive. Why did this happen?**

A: When you stopped your study with the Traveler (called reading Discourses), you began dropping your end of the initiation. When an initiate drops their end, the Traveler drops his end, since the Traveler does not inflict on anyone and respects their choices. Gradually, the person's tone goes inactive, and this usually happens when an initiate has allowed their Discourse subscription to expire for over six months. (This also applies to the subscription to Soul Awareness Tapes—SAT—when a person has completed the twelve years of Discourses.) When the tone goes inactive, it's a little like a battery running down and not having any energy. It can take some time of reading Discourses and doing s.e.'s to get the battery (tone) active again when it has gone inactive. The person's initiation tones will be reactivated as the person moves up the levels, and it will be done spiritually as it matches their intention.

The guideline is that if a person stops reading Discourses for 1-1/2 years or more, they need to start over again on their Discourse reading, beginning with Discourse 1. When they are rereading Discourse 25 (two years of studying the Discourses again), they can check back and see if their tone is active again. Is studying the Discourses just a technicality? In a way, yes, but it's a necessary one. It is for the discipline of all of us to hold the initiations once they have been given.

Discourses are a point of attunement with the Traveler, as well as an initiate's study with the Traveler. (This also applies to the Soul Awareness Tapes after a person has completed the twelve years of Discourses.) Some people have thought that they could just order the Discourses and not actually read them and still remain "active." Sure, they are active on the MSIA mailing list and counted as active in terms of attending MSIA events, but in the spiritual realms, where it really counts, are they active? Maybe, and maybe not. I've initiated a lot of people, but not all of them are initiates.

**Q: So, when I have finished rereading Discourse 25, will I be reinitiated?**

A: There is no reinitiation if you have received initiation before. It is a process of your initiation tone becoming active again.

**Q: I was an initiate in MSIA many years ago and then stopped for several years. During the time I was not moving in MSIA circles, I spent memorable time with you in the dream state.**

**Does this have any bearing on the reactivation of my initiation?**

A: No. I spend time spiritually with many who are not in the outward MSIA. They are being prepared for further evolution.

## Q&A About the Initiation Tone

**Q: I have heard that there is more than one Sound Current. Is this accurate?**

A: There is the Sound Current, the basis of all life. Others may call something the Sound Current, and it may or may not be that. Some sounds are more directly reflective of or in harmony with the Sound Current of God than others. The tones chanted in MSIA and your initiation tones are in close harmony with the Sound Current of God.

**Q: When I chant my initiation tone, which is saying the names of the Lords of the astral and causal realms, I feel like I'm praying to lesser Gods, not the Supreme God. Does chanting the names of the Lords on the different realms violate the principle of worshiping one and only one God?**

A: No. Only the Supreme God is worshiped in MSIA. When you chant your initiation tone, you are not praying to or worshiping the Lord of the realm.

ध्

When you chant the names of God, as given to you by Spirit at the times of initiation, you are invoking the frequency behind those names. Each sacred name you chant reflects the essence, and therein lies the power.

Your ultimate goal is the Supreme God. The Lord of the realm is like a mayor of a town or area you're passing through on your way to God's castle. You need to go through fields, mountains, gorges, deserts, etc., in the mayor's province. Chanting the name of the Lord of that realm helps you go through that area in the most direct way possible. And, of course, the Traveler is your companion on the trip, too.

**Q: What does it mean when you say that my initiation tone is "charged" for my frequency?**

A: You have a unique energy vibration, as does everyone. When you were initiated, the Traveler spiritually charged the tone, which could be seen as putting "spiritual life" into it. (Otherwise, the words would be just words.) The Traveler also adjusts, or "tweaks," the vibration so that it is in harmony with your personal vibration and becomes *your* tone on a very personal level. No one else's tone vibrates at that same frequency.

**Q: I haven't been chanting my tone much, and I'm wondering if this is hurting my spiritual progression.**

A: Your spiritual progression is based on a Mystical Traveler helping you clear karma in the spiritual realms. Chanting your tone (doing s.e.'s) is for you to become more aware of this work.

ॐ

*There is an inner society that exists among the initiates of the Sound Current. It is a great inner society. We are all in contact with other initiates all over the world and in worlds beyond.*

When initiates of the Traveler chant, they chant for all initiates. So when one of us isn't doing our part, the Traveler's initiates may be chanting partly for that person. I'd suggest that you chant your tone so that you can know that you are doing your part for yourself. Also, I chant the tones for each of my initiates if they don't chant, unless they make it known to me that they want nothing to do with me.

**Q: I am moving on from MSIA and return my tone to you. May I meditate on it until I am given another one, or is it better to let it go now?**

A: Once you have let the tones go, they go. Each tone is built on the next one. Once you let go of the tones and the connection to the Traveler who initiated you, it can be difficult to reconnect them. Haven't you got it clear how much karma has been cleared from you already in this lifetime? Well, if you haven't, you will have the rest of your life to think about it.

The tone will work for a short period of time somewhat in relationship to how long you have had it and how well you have done spiritual exercises. You will be able to tell when it is starting to disconnect, as the negativity starts to move on the things that you may have found of value. At that time, pray for your Soul's strength to guide you. Don't

ध्रू

*Initiation is to the higher levels of Light. The more you chant your initiatory tone, the more you are affected inside. Some of the changes will be so subtle that you might not even notice them at first. Then you might find that you are being of service more and more or that your attitude has changed.*

mistake something that may appear to be of simple value as being simplistic.

**Q: Can the initiation tone ever be used for anything on this physical level?**

A: Once there was a drought in a particular part of the world, and I gave the people there this technique for assisting. Stand together facing where you want the clouds to mass and have moisture in them for the "raining time." Then, while keeping your intention in mind, silently chant your initiation tone while your arms are outstretched towards the area. Five to fifteen minutes should be ample each and every time that it is done. It can be done as a group or individually when you feel like doing it. And you can mix these, i.e., in groups, then singles, and then groups again. Mixing or doing it one way—all is fine.

## Q&A About Initiation
## and Reincarnation

**Q: Does an initiate have to reincarnate?**

A: If a person has been initiated to, say, the mental realm and if the person dies physically, the Soul does not *have* to return to the physical, astral, or causal level. The Soul may *choose* to take on a physical body in order to have the great opportunity afforded by the physical realm: moving into the Soul realm directly from the physical level. Alternately, a Soul on the mental level in Spirit could also work through the mental level, move on to the etheric level and work through that level (we're talking eons here), and then move to the Soul level. It can be a straighter shot from the physical level to the Soul level. Only from the Soul level do you not *have* to reincarnate. Any other level below that is "reincarnation rag."

**Q: I'm afraid that if I don't move on a business venture that has come up for me, I will have to reincarnate because I won't be complete.**

A: That is not the reason for reincarnation. The reason for reincarnation is not being connected to the Sound Current.

**Q: Does one's ability to work off karma and break free of the wheel of incarnation improve with each new level of initiation above Soul?**

A: Yes, if the initiation is *maintained* until death occurs.

**Q: Assuming I maintain the Soul initiation until death, what actions, thoughts, etc., would earn me a return trip?**

A: If you maintain the Soul-level initiation, there would be very little, if anything, that you could do here that could "earn you a return trip," though turning from the Traveler and your initiations could do that.

**Q: When a person has been established in the Soul realm and if that person decides to come back and help somebody else get going spiritually, can that person blow it and need to incarnate again?**

A: Sure, anyone can fall. That's one reason why you walk very cautiously and why you say, "I'm not picking up your karma, love. Work it out yourself. I'll help you by staying here and encouraging you, but I'm not taking it."

## Q&A About Soul Initiation and Above

**Q: Does receiving the Soul initiation physically make it harder for me to maintain the physical level?**

A: Not necessarily.

**Q: Will getting the Soul initiation physically open a kind of Pandora's box and give me a lot of new issues to deal with?**

A: It doesn't necessarily open a Pandora's box, but it does mean that the Traveler's promise to take you to the Soul realm is now complete. After Soul initiation, you then get a chance to start clearing all the karma that was held back while the Traveler assisted you to move up through the levels to the Soul realm. If you do not turn from the Traveler, the Traveler who gave you the first initiation usually continues to work with you to clear karma on the lower levels.

**Q: What happens after Soul-level initiation?**
A: After Soul-level initiation, about 90 to 99 percent of all initiates will go back down into the lower levels and want to clear karma. Why? Because they have the omnipotence of God present with them, and a person can clear a lot of karma from the Soul level that they can't touch from the levels below the Soul.

Some Soul-level initiates want to go into the levels above Soul, and there are a lot of reasons for this. One is the ego: "I can tell people I've been initiated one or two levels above the Soul, and I'll be better and greater and wiser than the whole group." That's not true. That may be all you're going to do. And when the others die, they may go up a lot of levels higher than you because you may go just to the level of your last initiation.

If you receive and maintain the first Sound Current initiation above the Soul level, this secures the Soul-level initiation; put another way, it establishes you on the Soul level. Other than that, I would suggest that you not go for initiations above Soul level but that you go for clearing karma because that is what's holding you. It's not lack of initiations that holds you; it's too much karma. So when you can get high enough to clear karma below you, I'd suggest you just get busy. Be a real happy "eater."

**Q: Is it still all right to turn to the Traveler for protection after Soul-level initiation?**

A: Yes. You may be going down into the lower levels—astral, causal, mental, etheric, some sublevels—to work out karma. The Traveler will work with you and watch. But it's not the same way as it was before Soul-level initiation because you're pulling your own energy fields down through the lower levels. The Soul may seem to be "stupid" or "dumb" in that it doesn't discern that something may be too much, because it doesn't see *anything* as too much. So you have to lift to a higher level of awareness to say, "It's too much to keep at that. Move off into another level." And the Soul goes, "Oh, sure."

The Soul is so readily moveable and can be beguiled so easily. But the Traveler takes you up

धू

*Having an agreement to work with me above the Soul level means that you are working with a more refined energy. Clearing the karma from above Soul can be like dusting a glass; clearing it from a lower level is like having to break up granite.*

through the levels of consciousness and initiates you into mystery schools in the spiritual levels, where you're taught and shown the deceptions of the realms below the Soul. So when someone comes to you inwardly and says, "Come over here," maybe somebody else from a Traveler's mystery school comes and tells you, "Don't go at this time. You can go at a later time." That's like saying, "You know, you're going to lead yourself astray in this other level and build karma here, instead of dissolving it." We're not in the business of building karma.

Q: After Soul-level initiation, when I have questions or issues, may I still write to you about them, and may I still regard you as my spiritual teacher?

A: Sure, you can still write and ask questions about things.

Once you've been initiated to the Soul level, my agreement with you is technically over. When you got the causal initiation, I said, "If you don't turn from the Traveler, I'll stay with you to the Soul level." And so a lot of people get scared and say, "I don't want to get Soul-level initiation because I'll be abandoned." No, you won't. You'll be in a form of God consciousness more than you are now. You're in it here, but it's being restricted by a whole lot of conditioning around you. And as you get up higher, those conditions leave and you start to become aware of it.

I don't think you're going to have any fear on those higher levels because I've never seen it exist there. But when you come back down here and think about it, you may have some fear because you're creating it. So if you just say, "Well, good gravy, this is what I was going for; I'll take it and see what happens from there," then we may agree to work higher in the levels above the Soul realm.

After Soul-level initiation, it's almost as though nothing really changed. You may wonder, "Why was I so anxious?" It's because you were so anxious. There was no reason to be.

**Q: I have received Soul initiation, and you and I have not yet made an agreement to work together above the Soul level, so I must be clearing karma on the lower levels. This is okay with me, but I haven't felt connected to the Traveler, and I wonder if there is something going on here that you can tell me about.**

A: What you describe is rare, but it sometimes happens. You chose to work off karma in the lower levels without the assistance of a Traveler. This is one of those things that is decided on the inner levels, and it was both a result of karma and a clearing of karma. This is one of the reasons you haven't felt a sense of connectedness with the Traveler.

**Q: Is there anything I can do about this?**

A: Well, there is karma to clear, whether you like it or not, so you might as well approach it with a positive attitude, like, "Hey! I get to clear some karma here!" There's not much choice other than to keep on keeping on. And if your intention is to continue on with the Traveler when the karmic flow clears, then hold that as your focus.

**Q: You and I have an agreement to work together above the Soul level. How will I know if I have received any initiations above the Soul level, and do I come in to get initiated like I did for the other initiations?**

A: There is no pattern as to when above-Soul initiations take place; they happen when they happen. If you have any experiences that seem to indicate an initiation, you can write and ask me. Often, though, these initiations above the Soul realm are much more subtle than the ones below the Soul realm, and you may not bring back an experience consciously. If you do receive a Sound Current initiation above Soul, you do not come in for a physical initiation; it takes place on the spiritual levels.

Initiations above Soul take place even if a person is not aware of them, and there is no push to get them. They continue after a person leaves the body physically, and getting them in the physical lifetime is not more important than getting them after the physical lifetime.

Also, there are no more initiation tones given after Soul-level initiation. The five initiation tones (astral/causal, mental, etheric, and Soul tones) are enough to move a person into the heart of God, if that person gets a Mystical Traveler to take them up, and they are the only tones you need for traveling in the levels above Soul. There are many sounds in the levels of pure Spirit, but they do not work as transcendent sounds.

**Q: Do I have to give up Jesus Christ if I am working with you above the Soul level?**

A: No. The Christ energy and Jesus, as the one who manifested that consciousness so completely, are still available, and evoking them can be very powerful. This Christ energy is generally involved with spiritual work having to do with this planet and the levels up to and including the Soul realm.

**Q: I was a little surprised when a friend of mine, who had received Soul initiation, decided not to continue in MSIA.**

A: Many times, as we have seen, Soul initiates get the initiation and then leave. They won't stick around to help others.

**Q: Are there more challenges as a person learns to hold more Light or is initiated to higher levels?**

A: When you become a Light bearer, you become a focal point of struggle between the Holy Spirit and the negative forces. And the negative forces try to pull you off the path by doubt, fear, anger, frustration, avarice, jealousy—all the things that are negative. And this is why, if you've been dedicated and devoted, by the time you are traveling in the high realms of Light in this Movement, you'll be so staunch in your spiritual conviction that you can't be pulled off of it. If you haven't been dedicated and devoted, it can be harder for you.

**Q: You and I have an agreement to work above Soul together, and to tell the truth, I'd much rather just be there. I don't have the greatest attitude about being here. I feel like I'm in a cage (the physical body) and often feel angry. The best I can**

घू

*The Soul is everywhere. It's in the laughter. It's in the twinkle in the eyes. It's in the touch. It's in the empathy you experience when someone else is hurting. It's in the joy you experience when someone you love is happy. It's in all of that and more.*

do is acknowledge how I feel, turn it over to God,
and be willing to be willing to change.

A: How you are handling it is a good approach. In
a sense, the Soul *is* in a "cage" (the physical body), but
it's a cage that has been lovingly and freely chosen
before incarnation, even if you don't consciously
remember that. Each successive sheath surrounding
the Soul (etheric, mental, causal, astral, physical) is
increasingly dense matter. But the Soul still shines
brightly and does not judge any of it, since it is getting
the experiences it has chosen to get. When you feel
trapped, rather than hanging on to that feeling and
the suffering that can accompany it—called anger,
sadness, frustration, self-pity, etc.—you might try asking to see it through the eyes of your Soul.

## Q&A About Whom the Traveler Works With

Q: My boss is not in MSIA, and I put her in
the Light daily. Will the Traveler work with her?

A: The Traveler can work with people to the
extent that they invite and allow that; for the Traveler
to do anything other than that would be an infliction. So the Traveler will work with your boss as
much as she allows.

**Q: I am an initiate. Will the Traveler work with members of my family, and are they equivalent to me in terms of how the Traveler works with them?**

A: The Traveler may work with family members of initiates through the initiate. This is done at the level that the family member allows spiritually, because part of the nature of the Traveler Consciousness is that it does not inflict itself on anyone.

Family members of initiates are not automatically considered "equivalent" to initiates because there has not been the commitment between the person and the Mystical Traveler that is made at the time of causal initiation.

**Q: Doctors say that my father will soon pass over. I have talked to him a lot about you, and maybe with all of that, he got his astral initiation.**

A: That is true. Whenever an initiate mentions me, John Morton, or the Traveler to someone, that person gets the astral initiation very soon after that, most likely that same evening in the night travel. Your father benefits from your being an initiate and minister. It is, of course, all spiritual benefits, but then that is where he is going now. You will see him there in your own way, most likely while you are asleep, but it is not restricted to that.

## Q&A About Working with Other Spiritual Teachers

**Q: I would like to receive initiation in MSIA and also work with another spiritual teacher whose teachings ring true for me. Is it possible for me to do this?**

A: If you are a serious student of the inner teachings, it is imperative that you choose one spiritual teacher to study with. It is fine to change your mind if what you are doing doesn't work for you; however, it is not recommended that you have two spiritual teachers at the same time. In MSIA, this means that your spiritual teacher is John Morton or John-Roger if you are studying the Discourses towards initiation, are an initiate, want to be ordained, or are an ordained minister in MSIA.

If you try to work with two spiritual teachers, you will probably split your energy and not give yourself a fair chance, and you may even become very confused. In addition, you are not giving the spiritual teacher a fair chance of working with you.

People who are my initiates may be worked with spiritually by John Morton and vice versa. There is no conflict, as it is the Traveler Consciousness that is doing the spiritual work.

ह्रू

As you connect to the Sound Current, you are more open to receive the inner teachings. The inner teachings clarify and strengthen you in Spirit, and then you connect to the Sound Current on even higher levels.

Q: I am very attracted to a spiritual teacher in another country, and I am going there to study with him. May I have your spiritual protection on this new path I am taking, as well as your blessing?

A: You have my blessing and best wishes on your new path, because I support you and everyone in their choices. As for protection, your new teacher would be the one to turn to, as you have now chosen to work with this person. Whomever you study with should be able to protect you spiritually. If not, you might choose someone else.

## Q&A About the Traveler and Initiations

Q: When the Traveler Consciousness is held on the planet by someone who keeps the fact silent, how do people get initiated to the Sound Current?

A: Different Travelers have different spiritual missions depending upon the particular dispensation. Initiating individuals into the Sound Current may or may not be part of a Traveler's spiritual commitment. However, even if a Traveler were not known on the physical level (as many were not) and if spiritual initiations were to take place, there were agents of the particular Mystical Traveler who effected these

घू

*If you put yourself into the mainstream of the current of Light and Sound, God's energy will propel you. All you have to do is align yourself with Spirit, relax, and allow yourself to move with the energy of Light as it presents itself to you. There is a tendency for this energy to throw you out as it increases. In order to stay directly in the current, you must keep yourself directed into it.*

initiations, although it was always the Traveler who held the keys and line of initiation.

**Q: Do all Travelers initiate to the Soul level and above?**

A: There is a difference in the work of the individual Travelers. For example, some Travelers initiate people only into the causal realm, and so that Traveler needs to come only from the mental realm to do this. (It's not necessary for that Traveler to come from a realm higher than the mental realm to do this.) At this time, I am the only Traveler working with people above the Soul realm.

**Q: Do all Travelers have the keys to all levels above Soul?**

A: There are no keys above Soul, only ability and awareness of the levels of awareness (initiations).

**Q: I would like to study towards receiving the keys to the Traveler Consciousness.**

A: All the Sound Current initiates are in training to be Travelers at some time on one planet or another, so the training is already happening, virtually entirely on the spiritual levels. There is nothing else for you to do at this point physically because becoming the Traveler (in terms of anchoring the consciousness of the Traveler) is a spiritual action that then is manifested on the physical level.

## For More Information

*For an explanation of personal-use and public-use*
*MSIA materials, please see page 1.*

"Initiation—Molding the Golden Chalice" (Public CD #2601-CD). The key seminar about studying towards initiation and being an initiate.

"Focus on the Transcendent" (Public audio seminar #2624). Information on initiation, some of the initiate's responsibilities, and the initiate's relationship with the Traveler inwardly and outwardly.

"God Is Intention" (Personal-use audio seminar #7354; personal-use video seminar #V-7354). The basic seminar about the crucial importance of intention.

"Nine Times Around the Triangle" (SAT #7346). About the levels above the Soul realm and how what you do here can affect your Soul Transcendence.

"What Is Proper Spiritual Behavior?" (Public audio seminar #7343; public video seminar #V-7343). A close look at how what we do might affect us spiritually.

"The Sound Current: The Road Home" (Personal-use audio seminar #7493; English with French translation). A terrific overview of MSIA and initiation.

"The Divine Communion" (Personal-use audio seminar #3212). A beautiful seminar about knowing God, partaking of the divine communion, and knowing the joy of Spirit.

Initiates Seminars. If you are an active initiate in MSIA, you may get CDs of Initiates Meetings held by John-Roger. They have timeless information that can be a real wake-up call.

# APPENDIX 1

# FREE-FORM WRITING

The unconscious is one of our most powerful influences because, by its very nature, we cannot be aware of its influence until it surfaces. We may find ourselves thinking, feeling, and doing things that we cannot explain or experiencing illness or pain with an unknown cause. The vastness of the unconscious is impossible to fully explore. It marks the division between our waking awareness and our true spiritual nature, and to become aware of our Soul, we have to cross that line into the unconscious. As we do so, we lose something of our daylight awareness. That is why so many people talk about their spiritual nature but so few are aware of it as a living experience.

For years, I have used free-form writing to help clear my unconscious. It is very simple to do. I have described below the way I approach it, a way I know works.

## How to Do Free-Form Writing

**1. Find a quiet place and sit down with a ballpoint pen and paper.**

I also recommend that you light a candle because as you write, emotional negativity may come up and release into the room. Since it tends to go towards flame, having a lit candle may keep the room clear and the negativity away from you.

**2. Allow a thought into your mind and transfer it into the pen and onto the paper.**

You may not even finish a sentence before the next thought comes up. For example, the thought "go to the restaurant together" arises. As you write "go to the," you may have another thought, so you start to write that next thought. You do not need to finish the first one. The next word or thought that comes up may be "help," and you may write "hlp." That is fine because you know what you mean by it and you do not have to worry about spelling (or punctuation). But do not write in shorthand because that was not the form through which the thoughts and images lodged in your subconscious or unconscious.

326

It is important that you do not do free-form writing on a computer or a typewriter, since typing it does not carry the same impact and there may be too much negative energy releasing for the type-writer or computer to handle. Also, do not do free-form writing on a chalkboard or white board and then erase it. The energy that you released may stay in the board itself.

Free-form writing is a kinesthetic activity. The neural impulses from the fingers are sent back to the brain so that the writing actually releases and records the patterns of the unconscious. I call them the "beach balls," those things we have suppressed for a long, long time and on which we have expended energy to keep under the surface. They can carry tremendous emotion. So at times you may end up writing very forcefully. That's why I recommend that you do not write with a pencil: the lead can break and you lose the flow.

In some instances, you will find yourself writing as fast as you can, and at other times you will be writing slowly. But throughout this process, you should be writing continuously because there are always thoughts in your mind—and you are to write them down, even if they are, "I don't know why I'm doing this. What should I write next? Hmmmm." And do not be concerned if only "junk" is coming up when you do free-form writing; this means that the free-form writing is working.

It is very important when doing free-form writing that you do not just let the pen write. That is automatic writing, a very different process, in which you may be giving over your consciousness to something outside of yourself. Free-form writing is *stream-of-consciousness* writing, where you just write whatever comes into your mind. You are not giving yourself over to anything in this process because you are in absolute control of what is happening. You also write with the hand that you normally write with, not your other hand; free-form writing is different from the technique of writing with the subdominant hand.

**3. When you get through writing, do not read it over. Rip up what you have written and either burn it or flush it down the toilet.**

Some people still feel the energy of what they have released even after they have burned (or flushed) the paper on which they did the free-form writing. It is important that you stop the process when you stop writing. Have a set amount of time to write, and when it is over, get up right away (mid-word if necessary), drink some water, move around, burn or flush what you have written right afterwards, and go on with something else. Also, do not go back in your mind to what you wrote or anything you went through or felt when you wrote it. Let it all go.

If you keep the paper, the lower levels of consciousness will hold on to the pattern, and the release will not happen. For the lower consciousness or the subconscious to release and let go of the things it has expressed, that paper must be destroyed. And after you have burned or flushed it, fill the empty space where the images and words were with loving and God. Do spiritual exercises, and allow the healing and the peace of Spirit to fill you.

After you have done free-form writing for any length of time, you may start to get some beautiful, inspirational, wonderful prose that you may want to keep, but when you are through with your session, you may forget where the beautiful writing was and want to read through what you wrote to find it. Do not do this because the energy and negativity that you released onto the paper can return to you if you reread it. Instead, as you are writing and thoughts are flowing through, take the pieces of paper on which you write the inspirational thoughts and set them aside, separate from the other writing. When you finish your session, rewrite the sections you want to keep. Then you can rip up and burn or flush all the original pages.

**4. Never share what you have written with anyone else.**

If necessary, lock your door while you do free-form writing. If someone knocks, do not feel obligated to answer. You can tell people, "If my door is locked and it says, 'Do not disturb,' stay away. I will probably be out in a couple of hours."

**5. Start slowly, but work up to writing for at least an hour.**

Actually, two hours per session of free-form writing is optimal. Each person is different, but to notice some real changes, I recommend doing free-form writing for a minimum of three times a week for a minimum of three months. With practice, you can get to the point where you can do this in fifteen minutes, but it will probably take you a year or so to get to that point. You can start by doing fifteen minutes at a time; then increase it, the idea being to work up to sessions of one or two hours. Don't let the fact that two hours is optimal get in your way. As with anything I suggest, try it out as best you can.

The first time people approach this, they usually sit down and think, "I wonder what I should write." Instead, they should be writing, "I wonder what I should write. . . . Gee, this sure is stupid. . . . I think this makes me look like a fool. . . . I feel like such a phony . . . run . . . can't . . . yes . . . the green elephant was there . . . no . . . the cows jumped . . . I can't . . . I don't know why I'm doing it." You will see a flow begin, and then all of a sudden it may become jumbled. You may think, "I wonder why I wrote 'green elephant.'" Don't start doing that. Instead, write, "I wonder why I wrote green elephant." The writing will open the mind again, and the repository of jumbled information that has been holding energy will start to release.

## The Effects of Free-Form Writing

As you do this technique, a wonderful thing can take place. Because your free-form writing is often a symbol of an inner disturbance, you may find that pressure leaves you as you write. Obsessive behavior or habitual patterns may suddenly disappear, and you won't even know what it was that was inside you or how it managed to get there. You will just know that it is gone. Often, it will feel like relief or a sense that somebody has taken a weight off you. The strange thing is that you will probably not be aware that it was there until it is gone. Such is the nature of the unconscious.

When it goes, I would strongly advise that you not even question what it was because you might find it and reestablish it inside. We are powerful creators. Just by thinking about how glad you are to be rid of it, you could reactivate your own memory of it and—poof!—it's in.

I emphasize this because it is very hard to get something out a second time. I am speaking from personal experience. I once relooked at something, and it took me fifteen years before I was able to clear it again. I was aware every day that I had not cleared it, so I just kept at it. And one day it went. I knew what it was when it released because of where it was expressing in my body. And I just smiled and got busy doing something else to distract my mind so I would not go back to see if I had really released it.

There is something crazy about our human minds. We say, "But is it really gone?" And, in doing so, we can bring it back. It is as if we were to quit smoking and then smoke another cigarette just to see if we really quit. Then we are hooked again. My advice is that when you let anything go, do not be concerned about it. Just let it go.

I have seen some phenomenal things occur with free-form writing; it has released people from psychologically restrictive patterns and from physical and emotional pain. Free-form writing does not do a great deal for you spiritually, but if you are feeling clearer and better about yourself, there is a very good chance you will feel better about doing spiritual exercises, which *will* do things for you spiritually. With your unconscious free, you will be in a better position to be aware of your Spirit. As a stepping-stone to Soul awareness, free-form writing is wonderful.

When I see people grieving over the death of their loved ones, I can get drawn into it in negative ways. So I will spend a lot of time writing to free myself from this restriction. You can have a tremendous amount of empathy for others without letting their grief drag you under.

Free-form writing is like taking an onion and cutting a wedge through to the center. Then you leave a space, cut another wedge, and so on. If you leave the onion exposed to the air after cutting several wedges and do no more, the sections of onion that were between the wedges will dry up and peel away. And after a time there will be just a tiny seed

left. In the same way, by releasing some distur-
bances through free-form writing, others still inside
of you will fall away.

When, after free-form writing, you realize that
you had been carrying excessive weight or baggage,
rejoice in the feeling of freedom. When something
releases, immediately stand up, stretch, and move
around physically to experience your new freedom.
If you let the area get rigid and tense, you may have
another problem to deal with. You will often feel a
sense of diminishment taking place, as though you
are moving backwards inside of yourself, away from
things; they are getting smaller and smaller as you
move back. Don't be disturbed. That just means
that you are moving away from the materiality of
the world.

The CD set called *Living in Grace* has a CD that
explains free-form writing and, also, has music that
you can use as background to your free-form writing if you like. It is public CD set, ISBN: 978-1-
893020-38-2.

From *Webster's Ninth*
*New Collegiate Dictionary*

**Mystical**: **a**: *having a spiritual meaning or reality that is neither apparent to the senses nor obvious to the intelligence (the ~ food of the sacrament)* **b**: *involving or having the nature of an individual's direct subjective communion with God or ultimate reality (the ~ experience of the Inner Light).*

**Traveler**: **1**: *one that goes on a trip or journey* **2**: *an iron ring sliding along a rope, bar, or rod of a ship* **b**: *a rod on the deck on which such a ring slides* **3**: *any of various devices for handling something that is being transported laterally.*

**Consciousness**: **1** **a**: *the quality or state of being aware, especially of something within oneself* **b**: *the state or fact of being conscious of an external object, state, or fact* **c**: *awareness esp: concern for some social or political cause* **2**: *the state of being characterized by sensation, emotion, volition and thought: mind* **3**: *the totality of conscious states of an individual* **4**: *the normal state of conscious life* **5**: *the upper level of mental life of which the person is aware as contrasted with unconscious processes.*

# An Informal History of MSIA

## Pauli McGarry Sanderson

*Editor's note: In December 1988, J-R had held the consciousness of the Mystical Traveler for twenty-five years, and over one thousand people came to a gala dinner on December 18 to celebrate. Pauli Sanderson, who has worked with J-R since the early days and who was on the MSIA staff for many years, wrote an informal history of MSIA as an anniversary tribute.*

Think of the last 25 years of your life. Think of the variety of things you have done, the successes, the disappointments, the changes, the priorities you've had, etc. Think of holding one single focus for that amount of time. Perhaps you have, and so you know the process involved. Perhaps you're learning how to do that and can imagine what the process might be. J-R has held the focus of the Mystical Traveler Consciousness since 1963. He has said that he can forget a lot of things, but he never forgets he is the Traveler.

Tonight we celebrate and honor J-R, our beloved friend, and the work that he has done over the last 25 years. When I was asked to write something for this evening, I said, "Sure," and thought, "What could I possibly write that would do justice to the subject?" Then I decided that nothing could actually do justice to the subject, which gave me a lot more freedom. So join me as I take a walk through some of my memories, share some stories, and say to J-R, "Thank you," and "I love you," not just from me, but from all of us.

I remember, in about 1967, J-R and I went to Disneyland one evening. We went on the usual rides, ate the customary frozen bananas, played at the target ranges in Frontierland, and then, for a rest, hopped on the Santa Fe Railroad for a ride around the park.

Somewhere near the primeval forest, he began telling me about his relationship with Spirit and God, the spiritual awakening he had had in 1963, and the spiritual consciousness that was present with him. I don't know if he actually said "Mystical Traveler Consciousness" during that first conversation. I know he talked about being given a "special dispensation" in order to be of service to humanity. I know he talked about setting aside his life as an individual and dedicating himself to this service. I remember hearing clearly that personal preferences and his personal life were not going to be of much significance in this new work. I thought what a difficult choice that would be and then, as he talked more, realized that it was no choice at all and so, perhaps, not difficult. His joy of discovery and his enthusiasm for serving were so much greater than any seeming sacrifice.

J-R told me of his awakening to the reality of Spirit, of his communications with beings of Light (he referred to them as "the boys upstairs"), of his experience of other realms, and of the potential that everyone had to awaken to the Light and Spirit within themselves and in the outer realms. He spoke of how so many people were "sleeping," unaware of the Light, unaware of their own divinity. He spoke of how the veils of forgetfulness could be lifted from their eyes, if they would allow it. He spoke of the work he would be doing to assist people into that awakening and said that it would be "big." I don't know whether he knew the size or scope of the work, as it would unfold in the years to come. I don't think it mattered to him because all he had to do (then and now) was follow as Spirit led.

He told me of Spirit and the Light, of realms of existence, of ancient truths, of miracles and the mundane—all in the matter-of-fact manner of someone discussing what he had had for dinner the night before. I remember thinking clearly—some hours into this talk—that either this man was completely crazy or I was privileged and honored to be at the beginning of an absolutely wondrous adventure.

At that time, I had known J-R for about three years as a fellow teacher at Rosemead High School. We had laughed, joked, played, and talked about many things. I knew he wasn't crazy. I knew there was no deception in him; I knew he was good and honest and loving. So if he wasn't crazy, what he was saying was opening worlds and possibilities beyond anything I had ever dreamed of. Something inside of me sang, "Yes!" as he spoke. Silently, I asked, "Can I come, too?" His answer was, "If you would like to be a part of this and share the work, you're welcome."

This was how I first became aware of the Traveler and his work. I have been blessed to be part of the work. It has been every bit the wondrous adventure—and much, much more—that I thought it would be on that long-ago night. My experience, I'm sure, only differs somewhat in content from everyone's first moment of being awakened to the Mystical Traveler Consciousness and the joyful, affirmative inner response. From all of us, J-R, thank you for the awakening.

Through all of these years, I have been privileged and honored to watch this man we call J-R or John-Roger and the work that he has done—or perhaps it is the work that Spirit has done through him. Whichever way it is, he has consistently stepped aside in order to provide Spirit with a vehicle for Its work. Perhaps that is what the Mystical Traveler is: one who is willing to step aside and be that clear channel for Spirit, Light, the Supreme God to work through. One who will always make that choice. One who will not forget. One who will sacrifice, in the most joyful way, personal considerations and concerns for the greater good.

The work appeared to me to start small. J-R worked with people on a one-to-one basis. He counseled, he talked, he shared with them what he could see of their life paths, what they were here to learn and to discover, how best they could work with their own personality patterns, how they could awaken to Spirit and make it a part of their lives. As people talked with him, they awakened to new awarenesses about themselves and about the Spirit that was within them. Their lives worked better. They got value out of what J-R shared with them. They came back for more. They recommended others. People were experiencing the Light, finding out that they had power in their own lives, discovering that they could make choices that supported themselves and their families, awakening to the love that was inside of them, and learning to give and receive the loving in their lives.

In 1968, J-R was invited to share these teachings through seminars. Seminars provided a different format through which to talk about Spirit and the Light, and participants were able to experience these things in a very powerful and dynamic way. Because J-R could talk to more than one person at a time, seminars allowed the work of the Traveler on this physical level to grow. It began to pick up speed, and more people were learning about the Light and Spirit. More people were experiencing the movement of Spirit within themselves. More people were learning about loving.

People who discovered those first seminars in Santa Barbara asked J-R if he would do a seminar in their own towns. He said, "Yes," so there were more seminars. Sometime in 1968 or 1969, J-R's evening schedule began to look something like this: Monday evening, a seminar in Thousand Oaks; Tuesday evening, a seminar in Long Beach; Wednesday evening, a seminar in Thousand Oaks; Thursday evening, a seminar in Alhambra; Friday evening, a seminar in Santa Barbara; Saturday evening, a seminar in Los Angeles. His daytime schedule, of course, still included his regular teaching job from 8 a.m. to about 3:30 p.m. and private individual counseling from about 4 to 6 p.m. There was just enough time left for dinner and–on good days–"Star Trek" reruns before it was time to leave for the seminars. This kind of daily schedule falls under the heading of "service," even if–from the perspective of the many–it might look like it falls under a heading of "nuts." It was the physical manifestation of the inner direction to get the message of Spirit and Light to people. It was the Mystical Traveler Consciousness saying, "Yes."

Accompanying J-R on a great many of these evenings–and also seeing him during the day at work–left little doubt in my mind that there was absolute validity to his teachings about Light, loving, and service. He told us that if we are living in harmony with Spirit and doing the work of Spirit, Spirit will provide us with the energy needed. Energy is infinite. Spirit has the power. Human beings, in their earthly form, are limited. Those

343

limits are not so apparent when Spirit is present, when we give up our personal considerations, opinions, and judgments and open ourselves up to that which is for the highest good.

I watched it. I experienced it within myself to some extent. I saw it in J-R to a much greater extent. I listened to him give the same message over and over, in seminars, to individuals, to youngsters at school, to me. I watched all of us be pretty dense about receiving the message and putting it to work. Gradually, however, we caught on. Progress seemed sporadic. It didn't matter. J-R kept the same message present: Ask for the Light. Put the Light around you. Ask that those things which are for the highest good come forward to you. Be willing to accept that when you have placed something in the Light, what occurs is for the highest good. Love yourself. Love others. Take care of yourself. Take care of others. Use everything for your advancement.

The messages are simple. Applying them to life is sometimes simple and sometimes difficult. The teachings include perseverance. They include forgiving ourselves when we don't "hit the mark." The essence of the teachings is loving. And J-R is better at that than anyone I've ever known. Thanks, J-R, for all your loving perseverance, which is also called just hanging in there while we all do our best to follow your lead.

I remember one time, driving home from Santa Barbara after a seminar, J-R said, "Wouldn't it be wonderful if, years from now, people were living these truths and these teachings, and no one could remember where they came from?" I remember thinking, "It would be even more wonderful if they remembered where they came from." Now, I think maybe he was right. And I also think that he has accomplished what he wished for that night. I think of all the people, through all the years, who have touched in to the teachings—through MSIA, PTS, Insight, Baraka, the University of Santa Monica, and all the other programs that have sprung from the original source. I think of the people and how they have taken the ideas and energy of the Light and shared them with someone else, who may have told someone else, who may have told someone else, who may have. . . . I think of people who have, through a seminar or a retreat or a book, experienced a greater measure of loving and then have turned around and shared that loving with another individual, who got a sense that the world could be a more loving place, who in turn shared that with someone else. I do wonder how this has all moved through the world. In 25 years, there have been thousands of people who have experienced the Traveler's teachings; how many people have those people touched? Perhaps there are people everywhere living the truths and teachings without any memory of where they came from. Perhaps J-R has been successful in making that wish come true.

In 1969, however, the physical part of his work was still on a smaller scale. He was doing six seminars a week and still teaching school during the day. There was obviously more work to be done. There were more people wanting to know about the teachings of the Traveler, not all of whom lived in Los Angeles, not all of whom were able to come to seminars. One summer day, after our very first MSIA Conference (which was attended by a grand total of slightly more than 80 people), J-R said, "You know, if we transcribed the tape of the Conference, we could type it up and give it to people who could not be here." Service. The ability to respond to people's needs. So with a little tape deck, a stop-start foot pedal, and a portable typewriter, the first transcript was typed.

People who came to the seminars in California began to tell their friends and relatives who lived elsewhere about J-R, about the Mystical Traveler, and about the teachings. Some came and attended the seminars as guests, and they asked if they could get seminars where they lived. Of course, the answer was, "We don't have seminars outside of southern California." But the need was there. So J-R explored how he could respond to these people, how he could be of service. He began taping his seminars and making copies of the tapes available. But some people didn't have tape players (remember, this is 1969 or so). So J-R said, "Wouldn't it be great if we could put the seminars in written form so that people could read them?" Discourses. The basic teachings of the Traveler. They were originally produced on an ancient (but affordable) IBM typewriter. It got the job done. The original run was about 30 copies, and there was great excitement the day J-R bought an electric stapler so the Discourses didn't have to be stapled together by hand. The end result, of course, was that people throughout the U.S. were able to read the teachings of the Traveler and begin their own journey of Soul Transcendence.

One night, we were going to a new seminar location. For some reason, we each took a car that night, and I was following J-R. He was driving a bit faster than he normally did, and I remember thinking that he must have been in a hurry. I also remember

blinking my eyes numerous times because I was seeing little flecks of light on the freeway, and I
thought my eyes were tired. When we got to the
destination and got out of the cars, he was laughing,
and he said, "Did you see the Light going ahead of
me? It was moving so fast, I could hardly keep up."
Suddenly, I knew that my eyes hadn't been playing
tricks on me. But more than that, it gave me awareness of how obedient the Traveler/J-R is to the Light
and its plan on this planet. He just follows where it
leads and does the work as it presents itself.

In that obedience, there is no blindness, however;
rather, there is great awareness and presence. I
remember when his parents were ill; the awareness,
the work, and the acceptance that I saw manifested
were magnificent beyond all my experience then.
J-R's parents were wonderful people. Loving, no-
nonsense people, fun to be with, filled with life and
humor. He loved them very much.

When his mother was first diagnosed with a
"terminal" illness, I watched J-R go to work, sending the Light nonstop around the clock, researching
the best care, the best nutrition, the best medica-
tion, etc. I can only imagine the work he must have
been doing on the higher levels of Light and Spirit;
I only know what I could see here. There was no

anger, no sense that the illness was unfair, just hard work to bring to her the greatest chance for life (on this level or another) that was possible. He did not push his opinions or his points of view. He honored her and empowered her to make the decisions, supporting her in every decision she made, loving her in every way. When she died, it was with grace and acceptance. I saw his sadness and his joy intermingled—reflections of the man and the Mystical Traveler.

A year after his mother died, when his father was dying to this earthly plane, I watched him do the same thing: loving his father, caring for him in all the difficult physical ways, being with him as a loving companion, allowing him to complete the experience of physical life as he saw it. One night, a few days before his father died, J-R sat with him and told him how blessed and honored he was to be his son and how much he loved him. It was the most beautiful example I have ever seen of "honor thy father and thy mother." At that moment, the teachings of the Traveler took on new life for me, as I was able to see that this man, John-Roger, lived what he taught—even in moments of deepest sadness and difficulty. He held back nothing. J-R was—and is—his teachings.

When his parents were gone, he said that he had—as the Mystical Traveler—completed what he needed to, fulfilled what was necessary. If he stayed and continued to do the spiritual work, it would be out of love. He stayed. The work expanded. His love manifested itself in his presence, his availability to all those who called themselves his students, his ability to respond to their needs . . . in so many ways.

J-R's work is difficult to describe in the words that we use for communication on this level. His work is an inner transformation. Many of you know the work he has done with you inwardly. You may be aware in ways you were not before. You may know yourself better; you may love yourself better. There may be a different reality in your life. There may be a fundamental sense of joy or of purpose that is different from before.

J-R's work—from what I've been able to see—is individually tailored for each person because each individual needs different things for his or her own awakening. I have seen him work with people who have had so many challenges in their lives and have dealt with so many difficult circumstances, seen him be so gentle and lift them with hope and the vision that they can discover a way to greater happiness and peace. It may be that his energy holds the vision for them until they can hold it for themselves, and, in time, it manifests on this level. I've seen him work with people who have many unrecognized and unacknowledged blessings in their lives and are, in their ignorance, complaining about their lot in life; I've seen him be so blunt and direct with them that they awaken to the good things that are present for them and decide that if they want more, they alone have the responsibility and the ability to create more. And so they do.

My sense of J-R and his work is that each one of us who knows him and is blessed to call himself or herself his student has an individual, special relationship with him. I believe that we all know a different J-R. I believe that the Traveler has an individual relationship with each of us. I believe the relationship changes as we grow and move upward in our own spiritual evolvement.

Let's go back to about 1971. Seminars still were several nights a week. Counseling with individuals was still happening during the days. (Teaching school was not; the teaching had expanded to a larger arena.) J-R had found that the work he was doing simply didn't fit in his one-bedroom apartment, so he had moved to a house with space for the office (there were now a couple of typewriters, tape recorders, a mimeograph machine, an electric stapler, and some tape duplicating equipment) and a couple of people to help operate it all. The house answered a need. The house was a response to the growth of the work.

About this time, another service was added—aura balances. In the seminars, the Traveler had been teaching us about energy fields and how they affect the body. Now it was time to extend to people a way to clear the individual auric field, to release themselves from those thoughts and feelings that had held them in bondage, to forgive themselves and others in order to gain greater freedom. With more people needing more services, it was necessary to add personnel. So the number of people on staff expanded to meet the need. Again, J-R responded to the needs of those he served as the Traveler. Response-ability.

Part of the response-ability that J-R has demonstrated for the last 25 years has been the traveling that he has done physically throughout the world. Way back, in 1964 and 1965, he would travel throughout the U.S. during the summers. He used to pack up his 1964 Mustang and, a day or two after school was out in the summer, head east. He usually got home the night before school started in the fall. I never heard much from him during those summers, but after he was home, he would tell me about clearing energies from various geographical areas, releasing karmic patterns that had been with the earth for many years. The point of view seemed to be that because he could do these things, he would do them. My sense was that he followed where the Light led him during those trips. And he did the work that was indicated.

For several years, he traveled alone. As he added some staff people to help with the work, they sometimes traveled with him. Later, the traveling expanded. As it became known to MSIAers outside of California that services (aura balances and, later, polarity balances and innerphasings) were available, he began getting requests to come to Miami, New York, Philadelphia, etc., to do seminars and services. He responded. At first the trips were relatively casual; not much preplanning was required. As time went on and requests came from more people in more towns, the response-ability also had to expand. In the response was the opportunity for more people to participate and discover their own response-ability to Spirit.

The traveling has expanded throughout the world, and now J-R sometimes travels with larger groups of people. Because of the collective power of their Light and loving consciousness, they are able to assist with work on the planet that is an expansion of what J-R did by himself in the early years. What a joyful way to serve the world. What a wonderful way to respond to the world's need for greater loving and Light.

As an aside, long before I heard of response-ability (the ability to respond), I was impressed with J-R's ability and, more than that, his willingness to respond. There were innumerable times when a request for this or that would reach him only a few hours before he was leaving to travel or had a major commitment. It would have been so easy—and justifiable—to say, "This reached me too late; I don't have the time right now. It will have to wait." He didn't. If the need was there, he responded. He made the time. He fit it in. I was often in a position of being in between J-R and a request coming from one of his students. I knew the times that, because of something that was happening in his own life, it would have been easier not to respond. He responded anyway. He was there. I've rousted him out of bed in South America when someone in Florida was in a crisis and needed him. I've called him in Australia, in the middle of an Insight seminar, to help put him in touch physically with someone in Los Angeles who had need of the Traveler's energy in a physical, concrete way. He has always responded, always put aside personal considerations, always been there. Sometimes people want to see or talk to him and they can't get through; their message may be to go within. When the need is really there, the channel is open. One week, not so long ago, I was experiencing a difficult time in my own life and feeling a bit depleted in energy and the spirit to carry on. I encountered J-R "by accident" three times in one week. Unusual? Not in terms of this marvelous being we call the Traveler. Response-ability—to the Traveler Consciousness, to Spirit and God, to his students. Perhaps, it's all the same. He has been telling us this for a long time now, hasn't he?

Back in 1972 and 1973, the Traveler's work was (and is) clearly to offer the spiritual teachings to those people open to it, to make available the path of Soul Transcendence to those who recognize it as their own. Advertising was something that never seemed to be of particular interest; things were growing fast enough on their own by word of mouth. But one day, J-R mentioned placing an ad in a little metaphysical magazine. It was a small ad, and it said, "If you would know the secret of Soul Transcendence, write for more information," and gave our address. For a long time, there was no response to the ad. And then one day, a letter came from Africa. A man wrote and asked for information. We sent him our introductory book and a one-page flier describing Discourses and some tapes. He wrote back to say that he was blessed and honored to have found J-R, "the one who is the Mystical Traveler." And he started receiving Discourses. Today, there are hundreds of MSIAers in Africa. All from one ad that ran for about three months.

In one of the early seminars, J-R did a meditation that seemed particularly beautiful to one young woman, who wanted to put it into a little book. So she produced *The Spiritual Promise* and had a large number of copies printed. It was placed with a distributing company as a way of, perhaps, reaching more people than those who were directly aware of MSIA. Sales were not spectacular, but a young man in Australia happened to receive the catalog from this distributing company. He sent for the book. Then he sent for more information, then for the Discourses, and then for tapes. And then he started telling his friends about J-R, the Traveler, the teachings. That was the first contact in Australia, and now there are thousands of people there in touch with the Traveler Consciousness.

As the years moved on, the Traveler Consciousness continued, through its own plan, to reach out, to expand, to touch more people. It reminds me of the lyrics of a Paul Simon song: "God only knows, God makes Its plan. The information's unavailable to the mortal man." The Traveler has its plan. The plan included Prana, the beautiful old building that MSIA purchased in 1974, which has been home for hundreds of students over the years. It is also headquarters for MSIA, PTS, and *The New Day Herald* (formerly the *Movement Newspaper*). Living together, working together, and playing together in the energy of Spirit is a wonderful way to experience the teachings in a very concentrated manner. At Prana, one learns to live the teachings—because living less than that can be quite uncomfortable there. Prana is a place of service for many people. It provides loving, support (on lots of levels), and discipline for people living there. At Prana, the teachings come alive in a way they may not in other living situations. The teachings cannot be just theory at Prana. It's the lab experience.

The Traveler's plan included retreats, another opportunity for people to live and experience the teachings, another lab experience. If J-R has been able to experience the energy of Spirit coming in and providing him with the strength and vitality necessary to do the Traveler's work, retreats allow many more of us to experience that, too. And projects that may have looked too big for the time and space given to them are completed with love, laughter, cooperation, and sweat, as Spirit has supported us. So much accomplished . . . so much fun.

Service. It's what J-R is all about. The Traveler serving us. Allowing us the experience of Spirit—not just in spiritual exercises but in work, play, and interpersonal relationships.

Ah! Spiritual exercises. Speaking of service. What a service s.e.'s have been to those of us who choose to do them. Who but our best friend would tell us about this wonderful technique, this amazing path to freedom, this great tool for awareness? Thanks, J-R. Spiritual exercises—a window into the higher realms. A way to put this world, and all its materiality, into perspective. A way to make real the other worlds—and all their loving Spirit. As I write this, I find myself experiencing a peacefulness, a sense of the perfect order of God's plan, of joy and safety. The words taper off. Years ago, on the Santa Fe Railroad, somewhere in the primeval forest of Disneyland, my heart sang "Yes!" as J-R told me of the Spirit and the work. Today, as I think back through the last 25 years, my heart still sings "Yes!" as I think, write, and feel about spiritual exercises and all that J-R's work is.

"Yes!" and "Thank you, beloved friend, beloved J-R, for sharing it all, for responding to the cry in each of us to go home to God, to know our own divinity, to love and be loved in the fullness of Spirit."

Somewhere around 1977, J-R said that he had taught us many things about the Spirit, that we were all catching on and learning well, but that we still didn't seem to be able to make our lives work in a way that was bringing a lot of happiness and fulfillment here on this level. So in 1978, he gave us Insight and said that it was the vehicle through which he would come to this earthly level and "do battle" for us. And then teach us how to do battle for ourselves, by showing us the tools for making the world work. Response-ability. Once again, J-R saw a need in us—and he responded. Gave us more. Greater service. Greater loving.

It's been over 10 years since Insight began. There have been seminars designed to help us with just about everything—our relationships, our abundance (financial and otherwise), our effectiveness in our work, becoming neutral, and so on.

The seminars work as we choose to work them, which could be said for everything that J-R has taught us. He's told us over and over that he teaches from his experience. If something works for him, he shares it with us. If we work it, great; if we don't, that's fine, too. His job seems to be to give us all the techniques and tools that he knows. And he is very good at his job.

I look at the work J-R does now. There are MSIA tape seminars throughout the world. There are programs of every kind—the educational programs of Insight and the University of Santa Monica, service projects sponsored by the Heartfelt Foundation, and the work done for peace and integrity through the Institute for Individual and World Peace and the Integrity Foundation. There are retreats and classes given through Peace Theological Seminary, and an MSIA ministerial network. J-R's work has expanded tremendously, and there are more people participating than even he, I think, ever envisioned. Maybe I'm wrong. Maybe he envisioned the entire planet participating in the oneness of the spiritual consciousness. Perhaps we are still at the beginning of the journey. I recently had the good fortune to play a part in one of what I call the Traveler's miracles—a wonderful change and upliftment in the consciousness of a man near and dear to me. When I had a chance to thank J-R for his work, he grinned, his eyes twinkled, and he said, "You ain't seen nothin' yet." Perhaps that is so for all of us on this journey of inner awareness. Perhaps it has only begun and we ain't seen nothin' yet.

Whatever it will be, it has been magnificent. In a world that too often seems characterized by broken dreams and disillusionment, it is terrific to be able to participate—for 25 years and counting—in a dream that is even more alive and full of promise today than it was when it began. To be able to watch and learn from a man who demonstrates in his own life the ideas and concepts that he teaches and who is willing and able to be a friend in the very best sense of that word.

So, to you, J-R, my best friend, thank you for all that you have been, all that you are, and all that you will be. My mind still frizzles when I try to encompass who and what you are—and the fact that you are my friend for all of time and eternity. Webster had it right when he said that "mystical" goes beyond the senses and intelligence.

I wrote the following poem a few months ago. I wrote it from me to you, J-R, but as I was writing this tribute, I thought it probably could be from any of us to you, so I close with it.

"Someday you'll know
  how much I love you,"
One day you said to me.
Years passed and I did not know
Though I hoped and longed to see.

Today I know us better
My heart, your heart, our dream . . .
Love beyond all worlds and words
Peace and joy supreme

The pieces fit together
The puzzle is no more
Our laughter fills the spaces
Love opens every door

"Someday you'll know
  how much I love you,"
I know you know I do
And now I say, from my heart of hearts,
Please know my love for you.

May God bless you, J-R, with love all ways.


In June 1988, J-R passed the keys to the Mystical
Traveler Consciousness to John Morton, saying that
the transition would be gradual and would be complete near December 1988. J-R, at that time, pledged
his support to John, saying, "I stand firmly behind

John, or in front of him, or wherever he wants me to stand." He also said that he continues to hold the keys to the Preceptor Consciousness. So . . . we move to the next step in God's divine plan, and we accept with joy the Father's will. The journey has been magnificent, the blessings already are (as J-R has taught us so well), so we know there are only greater things in store for us. And with that in mind, we give to John that place in our hearts that holds the Traveler in sacred love and see in him the willingness to serve and the ability to respond to Spirit's call. God bless you, John, and welcome.

# APPENDIX 3

# SOUL AWARENESS DISCOURSE TITLES

1. Introduction Into Light
2. Sending the Light
3. Realms of Light
4. Acceptance
5. The Law of Cause and Effect
6. Responsibility
7. Working Your 10 Percent
8. The Mystical Traveler Consciousness
9. The Neophyte and the Initiate
10. Overcoming Discouragement
11. Control
12. The Magnetic Light and the Holy Spirit
13. The Impersonal Perfect Self
14. Unlocking the Locks
15. Love
16. Responsible Creators
17. The Three Selves
18. Psychic Centers of the Body
19. Soul Realm Mock Up

46. Physical and Spiritual Spirituality
47. Controlling the Inner Environment
48. The Divine Love of the Spiritual Heart
49. The Inner Journey
50. Speak Kind Words
51. Universal Laws
52. Breaking Fixations
53. Happiness
54. Honesty
55. Spiritual Gifts
56. Watch, Listen, Think, and Do
57. The Illusion of Separation
58. Security, Sensation, and Authority
59. Consciousness Focusing
60. The Power of Living Love
61. Levels of Contempt
62. Ectoplasmic Aura
63. Manifesting the Unmanifest
64. Overcoming the Dilemma
65. The Center of Truth
66. Love, Devotion, and Responsibility
67. The Purification of the Prince
68. The Process of Prayer
69. The Garden Within
70. The Presence of God
71. The Freedom of Spirit

# GLOSSARY

**Akashic Records**. The vast spiritual records in which every Soul's entire experiences are recorded.

**Ani-Hu**. A chant used in MSIA. *Hu* is Sanskrit and is an ancient name for God, and *Ani* adds the quality of empathy.

**ascended masters**. Nonphysical beings of high spiritual development who are part of the spiritual hierarchy. May work out of any realm above the physical realm. See also spiritual hierarchy.

**astral realm**. The psychic, material realm above the physical realm. The realm of the imagination. Intertwines with the physical as a vibratory rate.

**astral travel**. Occurs when the consciousness leaves the physical body to travel in the astral realm.

**aura**. The electromagnetic energy field that surrounds the human body. Has color and movement.

371

**Baruch Bashan (bay-roosh´ bay-shan´).** Hebrew words meaning "the blessings already are." The blessings of Spirit exist in the here and now.

**basic self.** Has responsibility for bodily functions; maintains habits and the psychic centers of the physical body. Also known as the lower self. Handles prayers from the physical to the high self. See also conscious self and high self.

**Beloved.** The Soul; the God within.

**causal realm.** The psychic, material realm above the astral realm and below the mental realm. Intertwines somewhat with the physical realm as a vibratory rate.

**chakra.** A psychic center of the body.

**Christ Consciousness.** A universal consciousness of pure Spirit. Exists within each person through the Soul.

**Christ, office of the.** The Christ is a spiritual office, much like the presidency of the United States. Many people have filled that office, Jesus the Christ having filled it more fully than any other being. One of the highest offices in the realms of Light.

**conscious self**. The self that makes conscious choices. It is the "captain of the ship" in that it can override both the basic self and the high self. The self that comes in as a *tabula rasa*. See also basic self and high self.

**cosmic mirror.** The mirror at the top of the void, which is at the top of the etheric realm, just below the Soul realm. Everything that has not been cleared in the physical, astral, causal, and mental levels is projected onto the cosmic mirror.

**crown chakra**. The psychic center at the top of the head.

**devas.** Nonphysical beings from the devic kingdom that serve humankind by caring for the elements of nature. They support the proper functioning of all natural things on the planet.

**Discourses.** See Soul Awareness Discourses.

**dream master.** A spiritual master with whom the Mystical Traveler works and who assists one in balancing past actions while dreaming.

**etheric realm.** The psychic, material realm above the mental realm and below the Soul realm. Equated with the unconscious or subconscious level. Sometimes known as the esoteric realm.

**false self.** Can be thought of as the ego, the individualized personality that incorrectly perceives itself to be fundamentally separated from others and God.

**Great White Brotherhood.** Nonphysical spiritual beings working in service to mankind in the spiritual line of the Christ and Mystical Traveler. They can assist with spiritual clearing and upliftment.

**high self.** The self that functions as one's spiritual guardian, directing the conscious self towards those experiences that are for one's greatest spiritual progression. Has knowledge of the destiny pattern agreed upon before embodiment. See also basic self, conscious self, and Karmic Board.

**Holy Spirit.** The positive energy of Light and Sound that comes from the Supreme God. The life force that sustains everything in all creation. Often uses the magnetic Light through which to work on the psychic, material realms. Works only for the highest good. Is the third part of the Trinity or Godhead.

**Hu.** A "tone," or sound, that is an ancient name of the Supreme God. In Sanscrit: ॐ

**initiation.** In MSIA, the process of being connected to the Sound Current of God.

**initiation tone.** In MSIA, spiritually charged words given to an initiate in a Sound Current initiation. The name of the Lord of the realm into which the person is being initiated.

**inner levels/realms.** The astral, causal, mental, etheric, and Soul realms that exist within a person's consciousness. See also outer levels/realms.

**Inner Master.** The inner expression of the Mystical Traveler, existing within a person's consciousness.

**Kal power/Kal Niranjan.** The power of the Lord of all the negative realms. Has authority over the physical realm. Functions out of the causal realm.

**karma.** The law of cause and effect: as you sow, so shall you reap. The responsibility of each person for his or her actions. The law that directs and sometimes dominates a being's physical existence.

**Karmic Board.** A group of nonphysical spiritual masters who meet with a being before embodiment to assist in the planning of that being's spiritual journey on Earth. The Mystical Traveler has a function in this group.

**Light.** The energy of Spirit that pervades all realms of existence. Also refers to the Light of the Holy Spirit.

**light, magnetic.** The Light of God that functions in the psychic, material realms. Not as high as the Light of the Holy Spirit, and does not necessarily function for the highest good. See also Light and Holy Spirit.

**Light masters.** Nonphysical spiritual teachers who work on the psychic, material realms to assist people in their spiritual progression.

**line of the Travelers.** The line of spiritual energy extending from the Mystical Traveler Consciousness, in which the Mystical Traveler's students function.

**Lord of realm.** Each realm (physical, astral, causal, mental, etheric, and Soul) has a Lord that directs that realm. The Lord of a realm is subservient to the Lords of the realms above it. All of the Lords of the psychic, material realms are subservient to the Lord of all negative creation, which manifests as the Kal power. The Lord of the Soul realm has authority over all Lords of realms below the Soul realm, including the Kal power. See also Kal power.

**Lords of Karma.** See Karmic Board.

**masters of Light.** See Light masters.

**mental realm.** The psychic, material realm above the causal realm and below the etheric realm. Relates to the universal mind.

**Movement of Spiritual Inner Awareness (MSIA).** An organization whose major focus is to bring people into an awareness of Soul Transcendence. John-Roger is the founder.

**mystery schools.** Schools in Spirit, in which initiates receive training and instruction. Initiates of the Traveler Consciousness study in mystery schools that are under the Traveler's auspices.

**Mystical Traveler Consciousness.** An energy from the highest source of Light and Sound whose spiritual directive on Earth is awakening people to the awareness of the Soul. This consciousness always exists on the planet through a physical form.

**Naccal Records.** Spiritual records that precede the Akashic Records and which record all events from the beginning of time.

**negative realms.** See psychic, material realms.

*New Day Herald.* MSIA's bimonthly newspaper.

**90-percent level.** That part of a person's existence beyond the physical level; that is, one's existence on the astral, causal, mental, etheric, and Soul realms.

**Ocean of Love and Mercy.** Another term for Spirit on the Soul level and above.

**outer levels/realms.** The astral, causal, mental, etheric, and Soul realms above the Soul realm also exist outside a person's consciousness, but in a greater way. See also inner levels/realms.

**Peace Theological Seminary and College of Philosophy (PTS).** A private, nondenominational institution presenting the spiritual teachings of MSIA.

**physical realm.** The earth. The psychic, material realm in which a being lives with a physical body.

**positive realms.** The Soul realm and the 27 levels above the Soul realm. See also psychic, material realms.

**Preceptor Consciousness.** A spiritual energy of the highest source, which exists outside creation. It has manifested on the planet in a physical embodiment once every 25,000 to 28,000 years.

**psychic, material realms.** The five lower, negative realms; namely, the physical, astral, causal, mental, and etheric realms. See also positive realms.

**Rukmini canal.** An opening in the void at the top of the etheric realm through which a person moves in consciousness into the Soul realm.

**Sat Nam.** The Lord of the Soul realm. Sat Nam ("True Name") is also the first individualized expression of the higher God.

379

**SATs.** See Soul Awareness Tape (SAT series).

**seeding.** A form of prayer to God for something that one wants to manifest in the world. It is done by placing a "seed" with (giving an amount of money to) the source of one's spiritual teachings.

**s.e.'s.** See spiritual exercises.

**seminar.** A talk given by John-Roger or John Morton; also, an audiotape, CD, videotape, or DVD of a talk either of them has given.

**Soul.** The extension of God individualized within each human being. The basic element of human existence, forever connected to God. The indwelling Christ, the God within.

**Soul Awareness Discourses.** Booklets that students in MSIA read monthly as their spiritual study, for individual private and personal use only. They are an important part of the Traveler's teachings on the physical level.

**Soul Awareness Tape (SAT series).** Audiotapes or CDs of seminars given by John-Roger, for individual and private study only. They are an important part of the Traveler's teachings on the physical level.

**Soul consciousness.** A positive state of being. Once a person is established in Soul consciousness, he or she need no longer be bound or influenced by the lower levels of Light.

**Soul realm.** The realm above the etheric realm. The first of the positive realms and the true home of the Soul. The first level where the Soul is consciously aware of its true nature, its pure beingness, its oneness with God.

**Soul Transcendence.** The process of moving the consciousness beyond the psychic, material realms and into the Soul realm and beyond.

**Soul travel.** Traveling in Spirit to realms of consciousness other than the physical realm. Sometimes known as out-of-body experiences. This can be done in one's own inner realms or in the outer realms, the higher spiritual realms. See also inner levels/realms and outer levels/realms.

**Sound Current.** The audible energy that flows from God through all realms. The spiritual energy on which a person returns to the heart of God.

**Spirit**. The essence of creation. Infinite and eternal.

**spiritual exercises (s.e.'s).** Chanting the Hu, the Ani-Hu, or one's initiation tone. An active technique of bypassing the mind and emotions by using a spiritual tone to connect to the Sound Current. Assists a person in breaking through the illusions of the lower levels and eventually moving into Soul consciousness. See also initiation tone.

**spiritual eye.** The area in the center of the head, back from the center of the forehead. Used to see inwardly. Also called the third eye.

**spiritual hierarchy.** The nonphysical spiritual forces that oversee this planet and the other psychic, material realms.

**10-percent level.** The physical level of existence, as contrasted with the 90 percent of a person's existence that is beyond the physical realm. See also 90-percent level.

**third ear.** The unseen spiritual ear by which we listen inwardly and hear the Sound Current of God.

**third eye.** See spiritual eye.

*tisra til.* The area in the center of the head, back from the forehead. It is here that the Soul energy has its seat and the Soul energy gathers.

**tithing.** The spiritual practice of giving 10 percent of one's increase to God by giving it to the source of one's spiritual teachings.

**universal mind.** Located at the highest part of the etheric realm, at the division between the negative and positive realms. Gets its energy from the mental realm. The source of the individual mind.

**wheel of 84.** The reincarnation, reembodiment cycle.

# INDEX

Introductory Note: Pages in *italics* indicate glossary entries. Pages in **bold** indicate the main discussion for a topic. Slashes between page numbers indicate the same material duplicated in the different volumes.

Vol. 1, p. 1-383 • Vol. 2, p. 385-835 • Vol. 3, p. 837-1303

abundance, 985, 1140–1141,
 1143, 1147, 1153, 1155
acceptance. *See also* nonjudgment
 of all experience, 94, 120,
 150, 152, 185, 187, 574–575,
 600–601, 840, 927, 989,
 1019, 1045, 1065, 1078,
 1134, 1160
 and death/dying, 752
 Discourses on, 365/817/1285
 of emotions, 962
 and inner peace, 1034
 and karmic cycles, 127–128
 Nathanael as symbol of, 549
addictions, 954–955, 957, 959,
 **1175–1187**
adultery, 1109
afterlife. *See also* death and
 dying
 and animals, 773–774
 and individuality, 769
 initiate's experience, 737,
 740, 742, 744–745,
 747–748, 771
 MSIA as preparation for,
 730, 731
 nature of, 732, 767–773

 and Soul, 744, 745, 768
 and Spirit, 767, 770
 Traveler's role in, 751, 771,
 772
Akashic Records, 87, *371/823/
 1291,* 858–859
alcohol abuse, 1180–1181
aluminum foil for protection,
 866, 868
amends, making, 85, 921, 1131
analyticity, 939, 940
Andrew, disciple of Jesus, 530,
 531, 533, 535
angels
 angel of liberation (death),
 736–737, 739–741, 743–744
 Discourse about, 368/820/
 1288
 spiritual role of, 849–851
anger, uselessness of, 1215
Ani-Hu, *371/823/1291,* 397–398
animals and death/afterlife,
 773–774
apologizing and making
 amends, 85, 921, 1131
apostles. *See* disciples
*Aquarian Gospel of Jesus the Christ*
 (Levi), 468, 571

Vol. 1, p. 1-383 · Vol. 2, p. 385-835 · Vol. 3, p. 837-1303

FULFILLING YOUR SPIRITUAL PROMISE

Vol. 1, p. 1-383 • Vol. 2, p. 385-835 • Vol. 3, p. 837-1303

baptism, 705–706, 849, 851
Baruch Bashan, *372/824/1292,*
 687–688
basic self, **57, 58, 60, 61–62**
 and baptism, 705
 and conscious self, 63, 65–66
 definition, *372/824/1292*
 and dying, 752–753
 education of, 521
 and energy healing, 1170
 and karma, 769
 and levels of consciousness,
  514–515
 and male/female polarity, 82
 mirror communication
  with, 1119
 and multiple identities, 101
 and prayer, 520
 and promises/vows, 1091,
  1092–1093
 repository for, 100
 and Soul travel, 393
 talking to child's, 1118–1119
bedtime talks for children,
 1116–1117
bed-wetting, 1118
being, state of, 33, 99, 126, 1198
Beloved, 64, *372/824/1292,* 622,
 1237, 1240. *See also* Soul
Bible, John-Roger's study of,
 594–595
biblical references. *See also* Jesus
  Christ
 asking for what one wants,
  983, 985
 Christ Consciousness, 488,
  523–524

Christmas story, 479–481
coding in Bible, 515
creating one's own reality,
 159
creation as good, 4
creed of Travelers, 259
disciples, 528–563
and fasting, 1175
going with flow of
 experience, 1232
healing power of faith,
 565–566
Holy Spirit as Comforter, 468
humans as gods, 1239
J-R's study of Bible, 594–595
Kingdom of God as within,
 528
Light and Sound Current
 references, 47, 49, 269
nonjudgment, 1025
oneness with God, 514
prayer, 421, 517
Soul travel, 390
spiritual endurance, 1223
Traveler, 259
treating others as self, 4, 1224
Word as Sound Current, 49,
 269
worshiping God in Spirit, 22
birth and Soul's progress, 23,
 63, 88–89. *See also* incarnation
birth of Christ within, 501
blessings, 1075–1077, 1125–1127,
 1169, 1171–1173, 1175
"blessings already are" (Baruch
 Bashan), *372/824/1292,*
 687–688

I-4

INDEX

in nonphysical realms,
143–147, 163–164
physical realm's importance
in, 734
process of, 133, 135, 137
Soul's role in, 168
and Soul Transcendence,
209
and spiritual exercises, 877
Traveler's role in, 142, 155,
211, 217, 219, 225–231,
233, 245, 299, 419, 421,
687, 973
co-creating
and Earth experience, 80
and emotions, 912
and the God within, 160,
161
and incarnation, 99, 103
and karma, 157–161
and life purpose, 2
with Light, 177
colors of realms, 45–47
Comforter, 468
commitment
importance of, 261, 263, 958
individual responsibility for,
282, 293–294, 673
and initiation, 273–275,
277–279, 281, 282, 293–294
long-term partnerships,
1091–1092
and MSIA guidelines, 5
to peace, joy, and love, 1190
promises to others, 996–997,
1091, 1092–1093, 1151
to Soul, 157, 159, 568

Traveler's role in, 216, 281,
282
to upliftment, 258
communication
and asking for help, 167
and attitude, 924–925
balancing of mind/body/
emotions, 949–950
with basic self, 1119
Discourses on, 369/821/1289,
370/822/1290
importance of honesty in,
623, 920–924, 943, 978,
997, 1024, 1069–1071
interpreting spiritual,
878–887
and karma, 124, 139, 141
and mental energies,
931–932, 940–941, 943
and relationships, 1069, 1071
and spiritual exercises, 394
community, spiritual, 257,
368/820/1288
compassion. See also love/loving
and Ani-Hu, 398
for enemies, 1130
and karma, 141, 161
as key to spiritual living,
1227
and sharing of Light, 183
and suffering, 149, 1043,
1045, 1047
completion with others and
death, 752–753, 754
compulsions, 367/819/1287,
954–955, 957, 959, **1175–1187**
Conference, 346/798/1266

# INDEX

intuitive knowing, 854–855,
991
of joyfulness, 919
and new connections to
Spirit, 406
of spiritual communications,
877–887
in spiritual exercises,
413–415, 417
disciples, **528–563**
discipline
Discourses on, 366/818/1286,
367/819/1287, 368/820/1288
emotional, 524, 989
freedom through self-
discipline, 1035
and initiation, 295–296
living in grace, 1219
loving of self, 1211
mental, 53, 928, 930–931,
933, 946, 989
with money, 1138, 1142,
1143–1145, 1144
and raising consciousness,
453
sexual, 1106
in spiritual journey, 274
and working with Traveler,
252, 253, 255
discouragement, 365/817/1285,
**1051–1057**
Discourses. *See* Soul Awareness
Discourses
dishonesty, spiritual cost of,
920–921, 924
divination, 851–861, 863

divinity, knowing one's own,
368/820/1288, 420, 564, 981,
1217, 1229, 1237, 1240
divorce, 1123–1124
doctors, karmic influence of,
1170–1171
"don't hurt yourself and don't
hurt others." *See* kindness
doubt
and decision making, 693,
882, 985, 992
and learning, 28
and Thomas the disciple,
549, 551
as tool of inquiry, 413, 667,
669
Dream Hall, 768
dreaming, **713–727**. *See also*
Soul travel
astral realm, 25–26
awareness during, 226–227,
229, 724, 725
and children's Soul travel,
1113, 1115
clearing of karma during,
143, 230–231, 233, 717,
719, 722, 726, 727, 873, 876
initiation, 270, 291, 316
opening of spiritual eyes, 409
Soul recharging, 188
spiritual exercises, 395–396,
405, 429, 431, 447–448
and Traveler, 226–227, 229,
297, 717, 719, 721, 723, 725
visits to Soul realm, 22, 227,
229

INDEX

dream master, *373–374/
825–826/1293–1294*
drinking water as clearing
technique, 874
drugs, recreational, 273, 741,
842–843, 847, **1175–1187**

Earth
as classroom, 5, 28, 98,
151–155, 162, 975,
1034–1035, 1043
and co-creating, 80
and energy flow through
body, 909
and free choice, 486
races and incarnation, 85
and Soul, 78, 81–82, 101, 523
eating, 1168–1169, 1173–1175
ecumenical, MSIA as, 459, 471,
473, 656, 661, 663
educational resources, 701–702,
706–707
ego. *See also* personality
and afterlife, 769
being kind to, 1211
Discourses on, 366/818/1286
fears of transcendence, 966
and God, 1043
imbalances in, 981
and initiation, 306
and inner voice of mind, 877
as instrument of love, 1227
men vs. women, 164–165
misinterpretation of s.e.'s,
441
and neutrality, 1018, 1025,
1027

and parental roles, 1113
release of, 157, 159
and self-sacrifice, 539, 541
and suffering, 1041
and three selves, 67
embodiments, 79, 81–83, 85,
303–305. *See also* incarnation
emotions. *See also* causal realm;
joyfulness
balancing with mind/body,
915–917, 922, 929, 939,
943–950, 978
being true to one's
preferences, 985
challenge of negative, 864,
915–917, 965, 1030–1031,
1036–1039, 1051–1057,
1095, 1097, 1122–1125,
1213, 1215
directing, 524, 928, 989
and dreaming, 715
energy patterns of, 911–913,
915–921, 923–929
vs. feelings, 21
and free-form writing,
327/779/1247
grief, 733–734, 753–754,
768–769, 1097
guilt, 117–118, 156,
366/818/1286, 686,
1023–1037, 1103, 1187
illusions of, 925, 927, 1031
inner voice of, 884–885
and intuition, 129, 131
karma of, 115, 117, 122–123,
135, 715, 963–964
as learning tool, 920, 962

I-11

limitations of, 595
and living in the now, 944, 945
loving approach to, 1211
and loyalty to Soul, 961
purpose of, 912, 1034–1035
in relationships, 122–123, 923, 925, 927, 1099
vulnerabilities to curses, 875
withholding of, 1071
emotive body, 30
empathy, 141, 143–145, 333/785/1253, 398, 508, 1043. *See also* compassion
endurance, spiritual
focusing on spiritual goal, 1202
and karma, 127, 142
and living in grace, 1205–1206, 1219–1223
patience with process, 1204
physical realm quality, 51
and spiritual progress, 290, 1195, 1197
energy. *See also* Light/Light of the Holy Spirit; negative energies
all existence as fields of, 908
angels as holders of, 850
auras, 352/804/1272, *371/823/1291*, 703, 773–774, 867, 1179, 1181, 1182
as awakening agent, 140
body's patterns, 898–899, 901–903, 905, 907–911
chakras, *372/824/1292, 373/825/1293*, 393, 395, 398–399, 864–865

and chanting, 298, 299, 397
connection to Spirit, 402, 628, 701, 894, 902–903
conscious manipulation of, 871, 880, 910–911
Discourses on, 365/817/1285, 367/819/1287
drug-use interference with, 1177, 1179
emotional patterns, 911–913, 915–921, 923–929
expanding capacity for holding, 1001, 1003
Holy Land's vortex of, 485
infinite supply of, 343–344/795–796/1263–1264
mental patterns, 929–943
psychic, 25, 435, 437, 839, 841–845, 851–861, 863, 1179
and sexuality, 1104–1105, 1107–1108
Soul as unit of, 38
spiritual charging of Discourses, 684
and spiritual exercises, 433–436
subconscious patterns, 950–951, 954–957, 959
and three selves, 60
Traveler's role, 219, 221–222, 256–257, 684
unconscious patterns, 951, 953
energy healers, 1170
enlightenment through MSIA, 740–741

and initiation, 283, 285
in loving, 1225
and physical-level experi-
    ence, 486, 665–671, 981
in relationships, 1082, 1083,
    1096, 1122–1123
and responsibility, 575–576
and Traveler, 217, 315, 319,
    988
freedom. *See also* liberation
and being spiritual, 126
in clearing of karma, 142,
    168
Discourses on, 367/819/1287,
    368/820/1288
and free-form writing,
    334/786/1254
from illusions of physical
    level, 907
and initiation tone, 426
inner, 521–523, 1046
and learning from experi-
    ence, 1031, 1033, 1098
to live one's own life, 1096
and living in the now, 1092
through observation, 1035
in positive realms, 50
in relationships, 1232, 1239,
    1241
and responsibility, 575–576,
    997
in Soul consciousness, 713
and Soul Transcendence,
    556
through vigilance, 1219

free-form writing, 27, 137,
    **325–334/777–786/1245–1254,**
    876, 952
free will vs. free choice, 91

game, life as, 128–129,
    366/818/1286
garlic, J-R's allergy to, 629, 631
gestation and incarnation, 63,
    88–89
ghosts, 749, 842, 848
giving. *See* service
glory, 620, 708, 1231, 1233
God. *See also* co-creating
as in all things, 178, 595, 597,
    642, 670, 903, 1009, 1027,
    1056
as within, 54, 160, 161, 391,
    528, 902, 1186, 1191, 1239
and balancing of mind/body/
    emotions, 948
demands of path to, 1202
Discourses on, 367/819/1287,
    369/821/1289, 370/822/1290
and ego, 1043
and emotions, 912, 1036, 1037
Fatherhood of God, 682
Father-Mother God, 64,
    198–199, 577
and grace, 1191, 1193, 1231
and human consciousness,
    181
humans as extensions of,
    107, 512, 892, 1239
and Jesus, 466
and joyfulness, 902
knowing, 36, 983, 1003, 1193

mental energy-patterns,
929–943
subconscious and
unconscious, 950–954
unique relationship to God,
181
human rights, 370/822/1290
humility, Andrew as symbol
of, 533, 535
humor, 102, 138, 639, 1019,
1021, 1052, 1207, 1232
hurting others. *See* inflicting
against others; kindness

"I AM," 18, 41, 521
illnesses, 1038, 1165, 1167, 1169,
1171
illusion
Discourses on, 368/820/1288
in emotions, 925, 927, 1031
fears as, 1056
of lower realms, 96, 229,
420, 903, 905, 907, 1027
mental-level, 932
of projecting into future,
936
of separation, 240, 367/819/
1287, 368/820/1288, 917,
1191, 1193
and suffering, 1040
imagination, 714–715,
1115–1116. *See also* astral
realm
immortality, 729, 735–736,
1201
inaccessible realms, 43

incarnation, making choices
before, **87–88, 91–93, 100,
103**
conscious nature of, 76
and death/dying, 735, 761,
763
and free choice, 87–88,
91–93, 735, 761
high self's role in, 63, 87
and personal responsibility,
973
incarnation, **71–107**. *See also*
reincarnation
choices before, 87–88,
91–93, 100, 103
and etheric realm, 35
gestation, 63, 88–89
introduction, 71–75
multiple incarnations, 79,
81–83
and negative realms, 77–79
past lives, 93–95
and races on Earth, 85
reasons for, 75–77
and Soul, 23, 63, 72–75, 77,
83–85, 87–89, 99, 105
and three selves, 58
three selves' role in, 63,
88–89, 100–101
transcending cycle of, 86,
95, 96–97, 100–101, 103,
105
of Traveler, 213, 319, 321
"wheel of 84," 99
individuality, dropping of, 49,
107, 769
infinite supply, 1140

Traveler chanting for initiates, 301
initiators, 271, 294
inner and outer Kingdoms of Heaven, 388, 389
inner child vs. basic self, 62
innerdependence, 591
inner divinity. *See also* Soul
  God's presence in humans, 54, 160, 161, 391, 528, 902, 1186, 1191, 1239
  knowing one's own, 368/820/1288, 420, 564, 900, 981, 1217, 1229, 1237, 1240
  love as guide to, 10, 11, 241, 459
  and Traveler, 674, 1039
  and Traveler Consciousness, 448
inner freedom, 521–523, 1046
inner levels/realms, 350/802/1270, *375/827/1295*, 388–389. *See also* astral realm; causal realm; etheric realm; mental realm; Soul realm
Inner Master, 246, *375/827/1295*, 496, 505, 513–514, 590, 991, 993
Inner Mountain, 368/820/1288
inner peace, 1034, 1132, 1190
innerphasings, 353/805/1273, 703–704
inner Traveler, 369/821/1289, 628
inner vision, 370/822/1290, 412, 443

inner voices, 370/822/1290, 877–887, 1226
Insight Seminars, 359–360/811–812/1279–1280, 707
insomnia and astral realm, 25
Institute for Individual and World Peace, 707
integrity, 368/820/1288, 369/821/1289, 415, 417. *See also* commitment
intellect, 31, 932–933, 937. *See also* mind
intelligence, spiritual, 9, 22, 41, 370/822/1290
intent/intention
  awareness during dreams, 725
  of being Spirit, 1198
  clearing negativity, 872
  connection to Holy Spirit, 177, 179
  initiation progress, 277
  invocation of Light, 193, 195
  and living in grace, 1201–1203
  mental understanding of Spirit, 965
  and service, 1223
  wakefulness in s.e.'s, 448
intuition
  and decision making, 989–995
  and emotions, 129, 131
  and intelligence of Soul, 22, 41
  knowing what works, 423, 671, 993, 1029, 1173

FULFILLING YOUR SPIRITUAL PROMISE

Vol. 1, p. 1-383 · Vol. 2, p. 385-835 · Vol. 3, p. 837-1303

and Traveler, 241
trusting of, 602, 854–855, 991
involution as path to positive
realms, 450–451. *See also*
spiritual exercises

James, disciple of Jesus, 536,
537, 539, 541
James, son of Alphaeus,
disciple of Jesus, 552, 553, 555
Jehovah/Yahweh as Lord of
causal realm, 27, 29
Jesus Christ, **461–473, 479–493**.
*See also* Christ Consciousness
and changing of attitude,
1033
and Christ Consciousness,
466–473, 479–493,
523–524, 565–566, 569
and disciples, 528–563
example of, 1239
healing work, 565–566
and Holy Spirit, 562, 565
on humans as gods, 1239
on inner Kingdom of
Heaven, 388, 528
on judgment, 1025
and levels of consciousness,
514–515
and Light, 484, 487, 535
on loving God and others,
1069, 1224, 1227
and MSIA, 457–461, 645,
663–664
nature of, 467
oneness with God, 514

as Self of Man, 493–501
and Soul Transcendence,
389, 457, 459, 476, 604
and Soul travel, 390
spiritual work, 461–466
and Traveler, 473–477, 485
jobs and work, 755, 757–759,
**1151–1160,** 1169–1170
John-Roger, **587–647**
beginnings of spiritual
work, 593–595, 597–603
biography, informal, 337–363/
789–815/1257–1283
challenges of leadership for,
635–637, 641
continual chanting by, 429
on death and dying, 348–349/
800–801/1268–1269, 755,
772
and dream interpretation,
717
as educator, 627
evolvement of, 1221
handling of negative
publicity, 1131, 1133
health of, 628–629, 631
initiation role of, 309, 1159
and Jesus, 474–475
and John Morton, 249, 251,
362–363/814–815/1282–
1283
John-Roger's Challenge,
1190
and MSIA, 587–591, 613–623,
698–699
neutrality at 10-percent
level, 1155, 1157, 1159

I-22

commitment to work on,
261, 263
creation of, 112–118,
122–123, 131–135, 154,
155–157
cycles of, 127–129
definition, 134, *376/828/1296*
and desire, 1051
and Discourses, 676, 681, 683
and forgiveness, 114, 127,
141, 156–157, 469
fulfillment of, 131–135,
143–147
and inflicting on others, 59,
61, 92–93, 113–118
and initiation, 275, 277–279,
281, 291, 293
introduction, 111–112
J-R's experience of others',
627
and judgment, 117–118, 121,
469, 1015, 1029
karmic flow, 124, 129–131,
164–165
law of, 1083–1084, 1229, 1230
and living in the now, 686
and love, 127, 130, 141, 151,
153, 1091
and marriage, 1087, 1089–
1090, 1095, 1123
and masturbation, 1107
mental, 131, 135, 166,
963–967
and multiple embodiments,
91–92, 97
and negative energies, 44–45,
153, 631–632, 679, 876

and negative realms, 135,
230, 233
and personality, 67
and personal-use MSIA
materials, 678
protection from others',
870, 1170–1171
and psychic advice, 852, 859
and races of humans, 85
reasons for good/bad
events, 121, 147–151
and seeding, 1139, 1141
sharing of, 124–127, 163–164
and Soul initiation, 305–306,
308, 309–311
as Soul lessons, 81–82, 111,
162
Soul travel, 393, 395, 715, 717
and spiritual exercises, 135,
263, 428, 435, 437, 877
and suicide, 759–760, 763
and 10-percent level, 506,
971, 973, 980
Traveler's role in clearing,
299, 973
and work/job choices, 1157,
1159
Karmic Board, 87, 91,
*376/828/1296*
karmic darkness, 165
keys for universes, 219
kindness (not hurting self or
others)
and dealing with negativity,
885
Discourses on, 367/819/1287
and empathy, 1043

purpose of MSIA, 666
sexuality, 1102
source of experience, 415
three selves, 57–69
Traveler's role in, 976
levels within realms, 23, 271,
273
liberation, 52, 53, 82, 158, 304,
736–737, 739–741, 743–744,
1232. *See also* freedom
life force, 175, 598–599
Light bearers, 192–193, 313,
509, 510–513, 573, 579, 581
Light columns, 189–193, 190,
196, 197–198
Light initiation, 271, 273
Light/Light of the Holy Spirit,
**173–203**
availability of, 284
and awareness, 20, 64
being instrument of, 1241
for children's spiritual
protection, 1118
and Christ Consciousness,
489, 490–493, 507, 509,
526, 573, 575–576
columns of, 196, 197–198
and death/dying, 751, 758,
759
in decision making, 989, 991
definition, *376/828/1296*
and desires, 1048–1049
direct attunement to, 180
and discerning God's will,
987
Discourses on, 365/817/1285

and emotional challenges,
927, 929, 1097, 1215
and eternal now, 41
focusing on, 180, 320
and health, 1169
and initiation, 490–491
introduction, 173–177
and Jesus, 484, 487, 535
and J-R, 339/791/1259,
348/800/1268, 353/805/1273
karma-clearing role of, 870
vs. magnetic light, 177–180,
365/817/1285, *376/828/1296,*
908–911, 932, 933, 935
and mental energies, 933,
935, 943
openness to, 9, 182, 208, 287,
289, 399, 401
personal responsibility to
attune to, 180–181
as protection, 573, 719–721,
841, 848, 865–868, 871–873,
876, 933, 1157, 1159, 1183
and qualities of realms, 45,
46, 47
recognizing in others, 528
in relationships, 1081, 1089
sending, 182, 198, 202, 204,
572–573
sharing of, 183–184
and Soul, 204, 959, 961
and Sound Current,
281–282, 442
and spiritual exercises, 449
and Traveler, 226, 235, 237
working with, 184–189,
193–203, 895, 963

Light masters, *376/828/1296*
"light saber" method for
children's fears, 1115–1116
Light workers, 486
line of the Travelers,
*376/828/1296*
living free. *See also* freedom;
liberation
and attitude, 228, 1015–1021,
1034, 1035
coping with difficult
people, 1079
cultivating, 129
and focusing intent, 1203
and freedom, 521, 523
handling negative energies,
1129
and inner peace, 1034
and karma, 142, 155, 162, 168
and life on physical level, 978
and Light, 195, 510
in relationships, 1074, 1075,
1083, 1120
and Soul Transcendence, 228
and spiritual promise, 1241
Living In God's Holy Thoughts
(LIGHT), 179, 449
Logos and Christ, 460
Lords of Karma, 87, 91, *376/
828/1296*
Lords of spiritual realms, 27,
29, 35, 44, 297, 299, *377/829/
1297, 379/831/1299*
love/loving. *See also* acceptance;
compassion; relation-
ships; unconditional love

all experience, 94, 108, 150,
152, 600–601, 840, 1065,
1078, 1134
and awareness of oneness,
106
and Christ Consciousness,
496, 508, 511, 514
and death/dying, 732, 751,
757–759
and discipline, 254–255
Discourses on, 365/817/1285,
367/819/1287, 368/820/1288
and entrance to spiritual
realms, 446
and forgiveness, 732, 1068
free choice in, 1225
and God, 4, 986, 1065
and grace, 470, 1209–1213,
1227–1233
as guide to inner divinity,
10, 11, 241, 459
as guide to right living, 990,
992
and Jesus, 460, 483–485,
1069, 1224, 1227
and John the Beloved,
541–542
J-R's spiritual work, 344–345/
796–797/1264–1265, 587,
605, 609–610, 613, 623,
638, 643, 646
and karma, 127, 130, 141,
151, 153, 1091
and letting go, 1024
levels of human, 925, 927,
1100
limitlessness of, 576

FULFILLING YOUR SPIRITUAL PROMISE

Vol. 1, p. 1-383 · Vol. 2, p. 385-835 · Vol. 3, p. 837-1303

and Jesus, 457–461, 645,
663–664
and John-Roger, 587–591,
613–623, 698–699
leaving, 313, 664
ministry, 701, 755, 757–759,
764, 867, 1181–1182
and money, *380/832/1300,*
696–699
partnerships outside MSIA,
1089
physical vs. spiritual atten-
dance at events, 283
prayer lists, 201
as preparation for afterlife,
730
purpose of, 97, 207, 587–591,
588, 666, 668, 1195
on recreational drugs, 1176
and responsibility for self-
reliance, 589–591, 1153
retreats, 357–358/809–810/
1277–1278, 697–698, 1055,
1057
seminars, 342–343/794–795/
1262–1263, 347/799/1267,
*380/832/1300,* 697–698, 868
services overview, 703–705,
706–710
sharing about, 691–696
spiral symbolism, 16, 17,
616, 618-619, 621, 662
study materials, 1/385/837,
673–688, 691–696, 764–765
tenets of, 3–4, 655
and Traveler, 590, 653–654,
663–664, 688–691

and Traveler Consciousness,
337/789/1257, 338/790/
1258, 341/793/1261, 356–
358/808–810/1276–1278
and trusting one's own
experience, 9, 665–671
MSIA. *See* Movement of
Spiritual Inner Awareness
(MSIA)
multidimensional consciousness, 20, 170, 404–409, 725
muscle-testing, 861–862
mystery schools, *377–378/
829–830/1297–1298,* 660
mystical, definition of, 336/788/
1256
Mystical Traveler, **209–265**
afterlife, role in, 751, 771, 772
and animals, 774
and awakening, 233, 241,
245, 624
and awareness, 210, 1176,
1177
and Christ Consciousness,
473–477, 518
connection to, 310–311, 392
correspondence with,
688–691
and death/dying, 734, 735,
744, 745, 747–748, 760
Discourses on, 370/822/1290
and dreams/night travel,
226–227, 229, 297, 717,
719, 721, 723, 725
as emotional support, 1053
energy work, 219, 221–222,
256–257, 684

in every human, 246,
654–655
free choice in working
with, 217, 315, 319, 988
giving over to, 212–213,
237–239
and God, 248
and grace, 851–852
and gratitude attitude, 1209
guiding role of, 35, 41, 96,
235, 237, 239, 246, 446, 1193
helping you get what you
want, 217
and highest good, discernment of, 994
incarnations of, 213, 247,
319, 321–322, 415
individual relationship with
each person, 351/803/1271
initiation role of, 269, 275–
279, 281–282, 285, 294,
307, 309–310, 315–316,
319, 321–322, 977
and initiation tones, 299,
301, 303
inner nature of teachings,
236, 674, 680, 881–883,
973, 1039
introduction, 211–220
and Jesus, 473–477, 485
and John the Beloved, 475,
543
joyfulness as signature of,
108, 212
J-R as, 221–223, 234–235,
242–243, 256, 257,
350/802/1270, 609

karma-clearing role of, 142,
155, 211, 217, 219, 225–231,
233, 245, 299, 419, 421, 687
and life challenges, 630
and Light, 226, 235, 237
and loving, 212, 232, 260,
415, 417, 658, 723, 725,
1066, 1067, 1241
Moses as, 469
and MSIA, 590, 653–654,
663–664, 688–691
neutrality in physical
realm, 213, 216, 219, 279,
315–316, 415, 417, 881,
973, 975–976, 979, 1177
nonjudgment of, 207, 857,
858, 883
and other spiritual teachers,
317, 319
and psychics, 851–852,
853–854, 857
reality of, 625
and Soul, 210, 214, 220, 606,
976
and Soul Transcendence,
104, 254, 264, 604
Soul travel, role in, 393, 395,
396, 404
Spirit form, 233–235
and spiritual exercises, 213,
215, 392, 427, 437–438,
448, 861
and spiritual marriage, 1095
and spiritual realms, 17
and truth, 612
and unconscious, 951
women as, 247

and chanting, 1122
Discourses on, 369/821/1289
eternal presence of, 494
and focus on Spirit, 41, 771,
996
freedom of living in, 1092
importance of living in, 146,
153, 187–188, 686
and mind/emotions/body
match, 943–945
and release of past hurts,
146, 1214
taking conscious direction,
524, 997
nutrition and diet, 1168–1169,
1173–1175

objectivity, 1019. *See also*
attitude; neutrality;
observation
observation, 1014, **1015–1021**,
1035, 1037. *See also* attitude;
neutrality
obsessions, 954, 955, 957, 959
Ocean of Love and Mercy,
*378/830/1298,* 511. *See also*
positive realms
office of the Christ, *372–373/
824–825/1292–1293,* 460–461
oneness
of all humans, 234, 572, 917,
960, 1062, 1216
and Ani-Hu, 398
awareness of, 45, 106, 684–685
with Christ Consciousness,
488
Discourses on, 370/822/1290
and everlasting life, 756

with God, 107, 513–515,
684–685, 895
and karma, 141
and Light bearers, 511
and owning all aspects of
living, 1212
onion, J-R's allergy to, 629, 631
online resources, 707, 709–710
openness
to God, 1018
and initiation, 287, 289
lack of ego agendas in, 208
to new experience, 6, 9
to Sound Current, 318, 320
and spiritual exercises, 399,
401
opinionated consciousness,
366/818/1286
ordination in MSIA, 701
"oscillate" and clearing of
negative energies, 873
outer levels/realms, *378/830/
1298,* 388–389. *See also*
positive realms
out-of-body experiences,
381/833/1301, 603
overindulgence, 115, 117, 1068

pain during spiritual exercises,
432–433
paralysis during spiritual
exercises, 433
parenting, **1112–1119**, 1124
past, letting go of
and challenging childhoods,
1114
and forgiveness, 977

as illusion, 420, 903, 905, 907, 1027
and initiation, 270–271, 283, 286–287, 303, 305, 980
kindness in, 906, 971
and night travel, 716
progress in, 286–287, 289
protection techniques for, 863–875
qualities of, 51
Soul's role in, 37, 39, 81, 1043, 1045
and Soul Transcendence, 762, 980–981
sounds and colors of, 46, 47
Spirit as refuge from, 1027
taking care of self in, 906, 972
and Traveler, 213, 216, 219, 279, 315–316, 415, 417, 881, 973, 975–976, 979, 1177
and Traveler Consciousness, 239, 241, 250–253, 256, 262
working with Light in, 963
physicians, 1170–1171
polarity balances, 353/805/1273, 704–705
polluted environments, protection from, 1169
polygamy, 1109
positive and negative energies, 173–174, 1075–1077
positive realms, **18–19, 43–44**.
    *See also* Soul realm
    definition, *379/831/1299*
    freedom in, 50

incompleteness of creation in, 161
and initiation, 279, 305–315, 1095
karmic clearing in, 143–147, 163–164
and liberation, 52
and Light, 175, 177
methods for staying in, 450–451
and night travel, 718
qualities of, 53
sounds of, 46
Spirit as essence of, 42
and Traveler, 211, 225, 255
possession by entities, 842–845
possessiveness in relationships, 1075
poverty vow, J-R's, 698–699
Prana, 357/809/1277, 702
prayers
    and accepting God's will, 982, 987
    attitude in, 500
    for being loving, 1067
    cleaning up unanswered, 26–27
    and connection to Spirit, 387–388
    Discourses on, 367/819/1287
    food blessing, 1173, 1175
    for highest good, 502
    initiation tone as, 426
    J-R's, 644
    MSIA lists, 201
    power of, 421, 517
    seeding, *380/832/1300*, 765, 1139, 1141, 1153, 1155

INDEX

service, 339/791/1259, 343/795/
 1263, 358/810/1278, 366/818/
 1286, 690, 1223–1227
sexuality, 432, **1101–1110**
sharing
 and free-form writing,
  330/782/1250
 of MSIA study materials,
  678–679, 681
 of spiritual-exercise
  experiences, 431–432
sheaths, dropping of in death,
 749
silence, value of, 520
Silent Ones, 51
Simon the Zealot, disciple of
 Jesus, 554, 555, 557, 559
sin, definition, 465
Singh, Sawan, 625
skepticism, 939–940
slander, dealing with, 1015,
 **1125–1135**
smells, spiritual, 256–257, 439
smoking cigarettes, 1183, 1185
Son of man, Jesus as, 493, 495
Soul. *See also* Soul realm; Soul
  travel
 and afterlife, 744, 745, 768
 as always present, 284
 animal vs. human, 773
 awakening to, 578, 896
 awareness of, 20, 33, 77, 170,
  244, 1203
 and body, 23, 88–89, 389,
  899, 901, 1186
 and Christ Consciousness,
  464
 commitment to, 157, 159, 568

and death/dying, 733–735,
 749, 757, 763
definition, *380/832/1300*
Discourses on, 368/820/1288
and Earth, 5, 28, 78, 81–82,
 101, 151–155, 162, 523,
 1034–1035
as energy unit, 38
as extension of God, 849
and grace, 1084
and high self, 62
immortality of, 729, 736,
 1201
importance of experience
 for, 37, 78, 81–82, 84, 101,
 258, 314–315, 417–418,
 573, 575, 975, 1031, 1209
and incarnation, 23, 63,
 72–75, 77, 83–85, 87–89,
 99, 105
intelligence of, 22, 41
joyfulness of, 72, 188, 582–583
and karma, 81–82, 111, 162,
 168
love as focus of, 3, 40, 729,
 1086
loyalty to, 368/820/1288, 568,
 959–962, 1017
and mind, 31, 32
"names" of, 40
in negative realms, 230, 233
neutrality of, 39, 1021, 1029,
 1045
nonjudgmental nature of,
 1209, 1211
perfection of, 33, 99, 365/
 817/1285, 614–615, 998,
 1035

definition, *382/834/1302*
and desires, 985
difficulty of expressing,
605–606
discerning, 883–885
Discourses on, 369/821/1289,
370/822/1290
as essence of positive
realms, 42
focus on, 746, 1198
and God, 43–44, 105, 107
heart as conduit of, 885, 896
and Hu, 397
joyfulness of, 925
as key to self-transforma-
tion, 1221, 1223
liberation in, 1232
life as reflection of, 708
mental understanding of,
965
and negative energies, 873,
1054
neutrality of, 1000
and the now, 41, 771, 996
omnipresence of, 670
patience of, 1033
recreational drugs as barrier
to, 1175–1187
as refuge from physical
level, 1027
and Soul, 49, 105, 173, 581,
976, 1238
subtle quality of, 478
Traveler's Spirit form,
233–235
and unconscious, 951

and work/job conduct,
1151, 1153, 1156
spiritual exercises, **395, 396–453**
and afterlife preparation, 731
as attitude adjuster, 399,
401, 1016
and awareness, 13, 263, 265,
404–410, 417–421, 440
balancing of self with, 987
as clearing technique, 872,
877
closing eyes during, 427, 429
and communication, 394
and connection to Spirit,
886, 1195
and death/dying, 753
definition, *382/834/1302*
Discourses on, 369/821/1289
distractions during, 418–419,
425, 443–444
experiences during, 404–409,
429, 431–448
and free-form writing, 329/
781/1249, 333/785/1253
grounding after, 445
group, 418–419, 427
and handling discourage-
ment, 1051
and initiation, 275, 289, 1182
J-R's perspective on, 419,
622, 627
and karma, 135, 263, 428,
435, 437, 877
life as one spiritual exercise,
958
methods, 401–403, 421–429,
441

telepathic voices, 879–880
tenets and guidelines of MSIA,
3–4, 5, 655, 971, 1109
10-percent level, **971–1003**. *See
also* attitude; health; jobs
and work; money; rela-
tionships
decision making in, 989–995
definition, *382/834/1302*
and destiny, 981–988
Discourses on, 365/817/1285
introduction, 971–980
and karma, 506, 971, 973, 980
problems handling, 996–1003
tenth door (spiritual center),
921
Thaddaeus, disciple of Jesus,
552, 553, 555
third ear, *383/835/1303*, 513
third eye, *382/834/1302*,
409–413, 443, 743, 921
Thomas, disciple of Jesus, 548,
549, 551
thoughts. *See also* mind
creative power of, 933–936
instant transmission of, 203
need for critical thought,
667, 669
releasing negative, 864,
935–936
telepathic voices, 879–880
time
and embodiment intervals,
83, 85
and eternal now of Spirit,
41, 771

free-form writing session
duration, 330–331/
782–783/ 1250–1251
initiation process duration,
291, 293
*tisra til, 383/835/1303,* 432
tithing, *383/835/1303,* 1139,
1141, 1145
tones. *See also* chanting; initiation tone
Ani-Hu, *371/823/1291,*
397–398
E, 445, 720
Hu, 51, *375/827/1295,*
397–398, 429
overview, 397–398
transcendence. *See* Soul
Transcendence
transition (physical death),
739–740, 748–755, 757–759.
*See also* death and dying
Traveler. *See* Mystical Traveler
traveler, definition of, 336/788/
1256
true self. *See also* Soul
and Christ Consciousness,
459, 501–507, 509–510
discovery of, 98, 1192–1193
and letting go of past
actions, 132
living in accordance with,
1023
mind as servant of, 967
as source of bliss, 1178
and spiritual exercises, 408,
1193
and spiritual promise, 1237

truth. *See also* discernment;
    validation
Discourses on, 367/819/1287,
    370/822/1290
and freedom from physical
    illusion, 907
and impact of honesty, 923
and interpreting spiritual
    realms, 15
in personal experience, 7, 8,
    14, 71, 413–417, 614, 657,
    665–671, 747, 907
and Soul, 40, 938
and spiritual exercises, 414
subjectivity of, 593–594
and suffering, 1044
as Traveler's job, 612
twin Soul, 1087

ultimate, the, 76, 1232
unconditional love
    Christ Consciousness, 459
    God's, 983, 1073, 1075, 1210,
        1225
    and John the Beloved,
        541–542
    and living in grace, 1230
    in MSIA, 700
    struggling with, 1099
    Traveler's, 1241
unconscious, 325–334/777–786/
    1245–1254, 333, 368/820/1288,
    **951–954**. *See also* etheric
    realm
universal laws, 367/819/1287
universal mind, *383/835/1303*
University of Santa Monica,
    706

Unstruck Melodies of Spirit,
    446. *See also* Sound Current
"using everything for uplift-
    ment, growth, and
    learning"
and attitude, 1031, 1033, 1207
commitment to, 258
importance of, 3, 5
and negativity, 854
not using against others,
    1109
and 10-percent-level
    challenges, 971
and three selves, 58
Traveler's role in, 212, 220,
    224

validation. *See also* truth
experience as key to, 7, 8,
    14, 71
of inner voices, 877–887
and psychic advice, 853
in spiritual exercises,
    413–417, 438
Traveler's role, 861
veil of forgetfulness, 63, 67,
    339/791/1259
vibration, 17, 193, 298, 299, 397
vigilance, spiritual, 1218–1219
vortex, energy, in Holy Land,
    485
votaries, Traveler's commit-
    ment to, 216
vows/promises, 996–997, 1091,
    1092–1093, 1151

washing hands as clearing
    technique, 874